# Ravenscourt
## B·O·O·K·S
## Teacher's Guide

### The Unexpected

Books 1-8

*Making Gold*
*Born Dead: The Story of Gordon Parks*
*The Navel of the World*
*The Mountain Is on Fire!*
*Atlantis: Land of Mystery*
*Master of Disaster*
*The Legend of Sleepy Hollow*
*King Midas and the Golden Touch*

McGraw Hill SRA

*Columbus, OH*

SRAonline.com

McGraw Hill SRA

Copyright © 2008 by SRA/McGraw-Hill.

All rights reserved. No part of this publication may be reproduced or distributed in any form or by any means, or stored in a database or retrieval system, without the prior written consent of The McGraw-Hill Companies, Inc., including, but not limited to, network storage or transmission, or broadcast for distance learning.

Printed in the United States of America.

Send all inquiries to this address:
SRA/McGraw-Hill
4400 Easton Commons
Columbus, OH 43219


ISBN: 978-0-07-611313-2
MHID: 0-07-611313-2

2 3 4 5 6 7 8 9 MAL 13 12 11 10 09 08 07

The McGraw·Hill Companies

# Table of Contents

*Ravenscourt Books* .................................................. 1
**Reading and Fluency** .............................................. 2
**Using** *Ravenscourt Books* ....................................... 3
**Individual Progress Chart** ....................................... 8
**Fluency Graph** ..................................................... 9
**Book Summaries** ................................................... 10
*Making Gold* ......................................................... 12
    Answer Key ..................................................... 22
*Born Dead: The Story of Gordon Parks* ........................ 24
    Answer Key ..................................................... 34
*The Navel of the World* ........................................... 36
    Answer Key ..................................................... 46
*The Mountain Is on Fire!* ......................................... 48
    Answer Key ..................................................... 58
*Atlantis: Land of Mystery* ........................................ 60
    Answer Key ..................................................... 70
*Master of Disaster* ................................................. 72
    Answer Key ..................................................... 82
*The Legend of Sleepy Hollow* .................................... 84
    Answer Key ..................................................... 94
*King Midas and the Golden Touch* .............................. 96
    Answer Key ..................................................... 106
**Graphic Organizers** ............................................... 108

# Ravenscourt Books

## Placing Students

Written for middle school to young adult readers, *Ravenscourt Books* provides materials and activities for enhancing the comprehension and fluency of struggling readers. Each of these fiction and nonfiction selections is

- organized within themes that are both engaging and informative.
- built to provide students with additional opportunities to read independently.
- designed to provide frequent opportunities for reading to improve fluency and overall reading achievement.

Some teachers have found these selections align with the independent reading levels of students in the *Corrective Reading* program. Use the chart below to place your students in the appropriate set of *Ravenscourt Readers*.

|  | For students who have successfully completed | Reading level | Page count (average number of words per book) |
|---|---|---|---|
| Getting Started | Corrective Reading Decoding A* | 1 | 28 (800) |
| Discovery | Corrective Reading Comprehension A* | 2 | 28 (1,800) |
| Anything's Possible | Corrective Reading Decoding B1* | 2 | 28 (1,800) |
| The Unexpected | Corrective Reading Comprehension B1* | 2 | 28 (1,800) |
| Express Yourself | Corrective Reading Decoding B2* | 3 | 44 (4,200) |
| Overcoming Adversity | Corrective Reading Comprehension B2* | 3 | 44 (4,200) |
| Moving Forward | Corrective Reading Decoding C* Lesson 60 | 5 | 60 (7,500) |
| Reaching Goals | Corrective Reading Comprehension C* Lesson 60 | 5 | 60 (7,500) |

*or have attained comparable skills

## Components

The **Using *Ravenscourt Books*** section explains how to incorporate these components into an effective supplemental reading program.

### Chapter Books
- Include eight age-appropriate books in each set
- Feature fiction, nonfiction, and retold classics
- Present additional practice for essential vocabulary and decoding skills
- Provide fast-moving story lines for independent reading

### Fluency Audio CDs
- Model pronunciation, phrasing, intonation, and expression
- Assist students in improving their oral-reading fluency

### Evaluation and Tracking Software
- Motivates students by delivering activities electronically
- Scores, records, and tracks student progress

### Teacher's Guides
- Outline ways to use the series in your classroom
- Include comprehension activities, word lists, and fluency practice
- Provide prereading activities and postreading writing activities
- Address reading and language arts standards

## Online Support

Go to **SRAonline.com** and click on ***Ravenscourt Books*** for additional support and materials.

The Unexpected

# Reading and Fluency

## Reading

Reading is not simply decoding or word recognition; it is understanding the text. Students who read slowly or hesitantly are not able to concentrate on meaning.

## Fluency

Fluency bridges the gap between decoding and comprehension and characterizes proficient reading. Increased oral-reading fluency improves reading comprehension.

## Fluent and Nonfluent Readers

The chart below presents an easy way to compare fluent and nonfluent readers. If students have several of the listed characteristics of nonfluent readers, refer to the sections on *Assessing Fluency* and *Fluency Practice* in the **Using Ravenscourt Books** section that begins on page 3.

| A Fluent Reader | A Nonfluent Reader |
| --- | --- |
| Reads words accurately | Reads with omissions, pauses, mispronunciations, insertions, and substitutions |
| Decodes automatically | Reverses word order |
| Reads smoothly | Reads word-by-word, focusing on words |
| Reads at an appropriate rate | Reads slowly, hesitantly |
| Reads with expression and phrasing | Reads without expression; ignores punctuation |
| Reads with understanding of text | Reads with limited comprehension |
| Reads so text sounds like speech | Reads without natural intonation |

## Oral-Reading Fluency

Oral-reading fluency is the ability to read accurately, at an appropriate rate, and with good expression and phrasing. The foundation for oral-reading fluency is automatic word recognition and extensive practice with materials that are easy for the students to read.

Oral-reading fluency develops as a result of multiple opportunities to practice reading successfully. The primary strategy for developing oral-reading fluency is to provide extensive and frequent opportunities for students to read text with high levels of accuracy. This means that selected passages should be ones the students are able to read with at least 95 percent accuracy.

Repeated and monitored oral reading is an effective intervention strategy for students who do not read fluently. By reading the same passage a number of times, students become familiar with the words it contains and recognize the words automatically. This improves reading fluency and overall reading achievement. It also builds confidence and motivation—particularly when students chart their progress.

The minimum target oral-reading fluency rate is 60 *words read correctly per minute* (wcpm) for **Getting Started** and **Discovery,** 90 wcpm for **Anything's Possible** and **The Unexpected,** 130 wcpm for **Express Yourself** and **Overcoming Adversity,** and 150 wcpm for **Moving Forward** and **Reaching Goals.**

How to assess fluency, how to set realistic target rates, and how to practice fluency will be discussed in greater detail in the **Using Ravenscourt Books** section.

# Using *Ravenscourt Books*

## Grouping

Students who have completed *Comprehension B1* will have mastered the decoding skills and vocabulary necessary to independently read the stories in **The Unexpected.**

***Ravenscourt Books*** may be taught to the whole class, small groups, or pairs. Assign each student to a partner. Partners can do paired readings for fluency practice. The partners will read the same story at the same time. ***Ravenscourt Books*** may also be used for individual student reading.

## Scheduling

***Ravenscourt Books*** is intended to be used as a supplement to your core program and should be scheduled in addition to the regular lessons. Times to use the books include

- reading and language arts blocks,
- before- and after-school programs,
- summer school,
- and out-of-school reading with parental support.

### A Suggested Lesson Plan for *Ravenscourt Books*

| | |
|---|---|
| Part 1 | 1) Introduce the series, and help students select a book.<br>2) Assess students' initial oral-reading fluency by completing a "cold read" of one of the book's fluency passages. The **Fluency Passage** section can be found after the **Thinking and Writing** section for each book. (See *Assessing Fluency* on page 4.)<br>3) Have students complete the **Building Background** activities. |
| Part 2 | 1) Preteach the unfamiliar words for the first chapter in the **Word Lists** section of the *Teacher's Guide* for each book.<br>2) Have students read the title of the first chapter aloud.<br>3) Have students listen to a fluent reader read the first chapter as they follow along with the text.<br>4) Have student pairs take turns reading the chapter again.<br>5) Have students take the **Chapter Quiz.**<br>6) Have some students do repeated readings to improve oral-reading fluency.<br>7) Repeat Part 2 for subsequent chapters. |
| Part 3 | 1) Have students complete the **Thinking and Writing** section.<br>2) Take fluency scores, using the same fluency passage used in Part 1. Have students enter their scores on their **Fluency Graph.** |

## Selecting Books

The books in each set are leveled so students can start with any book in the set. However, students generally find contemporary fiction easier to read than nonfiction and retold classics.

On pages 10–11 you will find **Book Summaries** that give a brief outline of each book.

- If the book is a retold classic, information about the original author is included.
- If the book is a good tool for teaching a literary term, the term is explained. The teacher should teach the term before the students begin reading.
- The last section includes other resources—books, films, or Web sites—that contain related information. These resources can be used for extra credit, reports, projects, and so on. Evaluate all books, films, and Web sites to confirm appropriateness of the content prior to sharing these materials with students.

# Using Ravenscourt Books

## Introducing the Series

1. Write the series theme on the board.
   - Tell the students that the books in the set all relate in some way to this common theme.
   - Brainstorm ideas about the theme, and write the students' ideas on a large sheet of chart paper. Include words, topics, and types of stories related to the theme. Post this list for student reference.
2. The books in each set represent several genres—fiction, nonfiction, biography, science fiction, historical fiction, retold classics, and so on.
   - Ask the students to read the title and the summary on the back of the book they chose.
   - Have the students predict how their book relates to the theme.
   - If the book is nonfiction, ask the student to predict what kinds of questions it could answer.

## Whole-Class Instruction

The following sections are designed for whole-class instruction but may be modified for small groups or individual instruction.

Set up classes in the *Evaluation and Tracking Software,* or make a copy of the **Individual Progress Chart** for each student.

## Assessing Fluency

Make a class set of copies of the **Fluency Graph** on page 9 of the *Teacher's Guide.* Follow these steps to **ASSESS STUDENTS' INITIAL ORAL-READING FLUENCY.**

1. Have the student read a passage that is set at the appropriate length (60–150 words) and at the appropriate instructional reading level (at least 95 percent accuracy).
   - The **Fluency Passage** section can be found after the **Thinking and Writing** section for each book.
2. Ask the student to do a one-minute reading of the unrehearsed passage.
3. Ask the student whether she or he is ready.
   - Then say: **Please begin.**
4. Follow along as the student reads.
   - When an error occurs, mark the error.
   - Count the following as errors: mispronunciations, omissions, substitutions, insertions, and failure to identify a word within three seconds.
   - Don't mark words the student self-corrects.
   - Don't mark off for proper nouns.
5. At the end of one minute, make a vertical line on the page after the last word read.
6. Count the number of words up to the last word read.
7. Subtract the number of errors to determine the wcpm.
8. Enter the number of words read correctly on the student's **Fluency Graph** by filling in the column to the appropriate number.
9. At the bottom of the graph, circle the number of errors made.
10. Review any words the student missed and provide practice on those words. The minimum goals for fluency are the following:
    - The goal for students who have completed *Decoding A* or have equivalent skills is to read the books in **Getting Started** at a minimum rate of 60 wcpm.
    - The goal for students who have completed *Comprehension A* or have equivalent skills is to read the books in **Discovery** at a minimum rate of 60 wcpm.
    - The goal for students who have completed *Decoding B1* or have equivalent skills is to read the books in **Anything's Possible** at a minimum rate of 90 wcpm.
    - The goal for students who have completed *Comprehension B1* or have equivalent skills is to read the books in **The Unexpected** at a minimum rate of 90 wcpm.

# Using Ravenscourt Books

- The goal for students who have completed *Decoding B2* or have equivalent skills is to read the books in **Express Yourself** at a minimum rate of 130 wcpm.
- The goal for students who have completed *Comprehension B2* or have equivalent skills is to read the books in **Overcoming Adversity** at a minimum rate of 130 wcpm.
- The goal for students who have completed Lesson 60 of *Decoding C* or have equivalent skills is to read the books in **Moving Forward** at a minimum rate of 150 wcpm.
- The goal for students who have completed Lesson 60 of *Comprehension C* or have equivalent skills is to read the books in **Reaching Goals** at a minimum rate of 150 wcpm.

## Word Lists

Follow this procedure to preteach the words for each chapter of every book.

1. Provide students with a copy of the **Word Lists** page, or copy the words onto the board. Underline word parts if appropriate.
2. Begin with *Proper Nouns* by saying:
   - **These are the names of important people and places in Chapter 1.**
   - **Touch the first word in the column.**
   - Point to an underlined word part (if necessary) and say: **What sound?** (Signal.)
   - **What word?** (Signal.)
   - (Repeat until firm.)
3. For difficult and irregular words, say:
   - **Touch the word.**
   - **The word is _____.** (Signal.)
   - **What word?** (Signal.)
   - **Spell _____.** (Signal for each letter.)
   - **What word?** (Signal.)
   - (Repeat until firm.)

4. Follow the same procedure with *Unfamiliar Words*. Discuss the meanings of the words. Use the words in sentences as needed. The *Word Meanings* category is comprised of the words used in the *Word Meanings* section of **Building Background,** so some of the words may be familiar. Only use the following procedure for unfamiliar words.
   - Point to each unfamiliar word, say the word, and then say **What does _____ mean?** (Call on individual students.)
   - (Repeat until firm.)

## Building Background

Use the **Building Background** section in the *Teacher's Guide* or on the *Evaluation and Tracking Software.* You can use this section as a whole-class activity or as an independent activity.

## Whole-Class Activity

1. Divide the students into small groups. Hand out copies of the **Building Background** page for that book.
2. Read the questions in the *What You Know* section. Have the groups discuss the questions and write an answer for them. Have a member of each group read the group's answers to the class.
3. Read the words in the *Word Meanings* section.
   - Then read the directions and go over each question with the students and say, **Which word best answers this question?** (Call on individual students.)
   - Repeat this procedure for all of the words. (Note: If the directions indicate that the questions should be answered once the words have been introduced in the book, go over each word again after the students have read the word in context and have them answer the question associated with that word.)
4. Collect the papers and score them based on the number of correct answers. Refer to the **Answer Key** for each book.

# Using Ravenscourt Books

## Independent Activity

1. Hand out copies of the **Building Background** page. Have students take turns reading each question in the *What You Know* section. Have students write their answers before proceeding to the next question.
2. Have students read the words in the *Word Meanings* section. Then have them read the directions and complete the section.
    - When students are finished, collect the papers and score them based on completion and effort. Refer to the **Answer Key** for each book.

The teacher may enter the scores on the **Individual Progress Chart** found in the *Teacher's Guide* or on the *Evaluation and Tracking Software.*

## Reading the Chapter

First, the students listen to a fluent reader read the chapter. The fluency model may be the teacher, a parent, a tutor, a teacher's aide, a peer, or the *Fluency Audio CDs.* Students read along, tracking the text with their fingers. Next, students take turns reading the chapter with their peer partner. An individual student reads aloud to the teacher, tutor, or parent, who gives feedback, points out missed words, and models, using punctuation, to improve expressive reading.

## Chapter Quiz

After the second reading of the chapter, the student takes the **Chapter Quiz.** The quizzes have multiple-choice, true-or-false, sequence, and short-answer questions. The chapter quizzes are available on the *Evaluation and Tracking Software* or as blackline masters in the *Teacher's Guide.* Use the **Answer Keys** to score the blackline masters and enter scores on the **Individual Progress Chart** found on page 8. The *Evaluation and Tracking Software* will automatically grade and record the scores for all non-short-answer questions for each **Chapter Quiz.**

Students should take each quiz once and do their best the first time. Students must score a minimum of 80 percent to continue. If the student does not score 80 percent, he or she should reread the chapter before retaking the quiz.

## Fluency Practice

Fluency practice improves comprehension. The teacher may choose different ways to practice fluency, depending on the student's needs. For students who are close to the target rate, have the student reread the whole chapter using one of these techniques:

- **Echo reading** A fluent reader reads a sentence aloud, and the student *echoes* it—repeats it with the same intonation and phrasing.
- **Unison or choral reading** A pair, group, or class reads a chapter aloud together.
- **Paired reading** The student reads a page aloud and receives feedback from his or her peer partner. Record the fluency scores on the **Fluency Graph** found in the *Teacher's Guide* or on the *Evaluation and Tracking Software.* Recording progress motivates student achievement.

For students who are significantly below the target rate, conduct **REPEATED READINGS TO IMPROVE ORAL-READING FLUENCY.** The student will reread the passages marked by asterisks in each of the books' chapters.

1. Set a target rate for the passage.
    - The target rate should be high enough to require the student to reread the passage several times.
    - A reasonable target rate is 40 percent higher than the baseline level.
    - For example, if the student initially reads the passage at a rate of 60 wcpm, the target rate for that passage would be 84 wcpm (**60** x .40 = 24; **60** + 24 = 84).

# Using Ravenscourt Books

2. Have the student listen to the passage read fluently by a skilled reader or on the corresponding *Fluency Audio CD* while following along, pointing to the words as they are read.
3. After listening to the fluency model, have the student reread the same passage aloud for one minute.
    - A partner listens and records errors but does not interrupt the reader during the one-minute timed reading.
    - If the student makes more than six errors, he or she should listen to the fluency model again.
4. The student should read the same passage three to five times during the session or until the target rate is met, whichever comes first.
    - After each rereading, the student records the wcpm on his or her **Fluency Graph.**
    - If the target rate is not met, have the student read the same passage again the next day.
    - If the target rate is met, the student repeats the procedure with the next chapter.

## Thinking and Writing

Many state assessments require students to produce extended writing about a story or an article they have read. Like **Building Background,** this section is not computer-scored and may be used in one of several ways. The *Think About It* section is intended to help students summarize what they have read and to relate the book to other books in the set, to the theme, or to the students' life experiences.

1. The questions in the *Think About It* section can be used for discussion.
    - Students discuss the questions in small groups and then write their individual responses on the blackline masters or using the *Evaluation and Tracking Software.*
    - The teacher may score the response using a variety of rubrics. For example, the teacher could give points for all reasonable responses in complete sentences that begin with a capital letter and end with appropriate punctuation.
2. For certain students, the teacher may ask the questions and prompt the student to give a thoughtful oral response.
3. Another option is to use *Think About It* as a mini-assessment. Have the students answer the questions independently on paper or using the *Evaluation and Tracking Software.*

The *Write About It* section gives students extended practice writing about what they have read. Students may write for as long as time allows.

The students may answer on the blackline master or use the *Evaluation and Tracking Software.* To motivate students, the *Evaluation and Tracking Software* includes a spelling checker and a variety of fonts and colors for students to choose from. This section is teacher-scored. Scores may be entered on a copy of the **Individual Progress Chart** or on the *Evaluation and Tracking Software.*

Students may keep their essays in a writing portfolio. At the end of the term students choose one of their essays to improve using the writing process. The final question in each *Write About It* section asks students to complete one of the graphic organizers that can be found as blackline masters in the back of this *Teacher's Guide* or on the *Evaluation and Tracking Software.* Graphic organizers are a structured, alternative writing experience. There are Book Report Forms, a What I Know/What I Learned Chart, a Sequencing Chart, and so on. Scores may be entered on the blackline master or *Evaluation and Tracking Software* version of the **Individual Progress Chart.**

# Individual Progress Chart

Name: _____  Class: _____

- Enter the percentage correct score for each quiz or activity.

| Book Title | Building Background | Chapter 1 Quiz | Chapter 2 Quiz | Chapter 3 Quiz | Chapter 4 Quiz | Chapter 5 Quiz | Chapter 6 Quiz | Thinking and Writing | Graphic Organizer |
|---|---|---|---|---|---|---|---|---|---|
| *Making Gold* | | | | | | | | | |
| *Born Dead: The Story of Gordon Parks* | | | | | | | | | |
| *The Navel of the World* | | | | | | | | | |
| *The Mountain Is on Fire!* | | | | | | | | | |
| *Atlantis: Land of Mystery* | | | | | | | | | |
| *Master of Disaster* | | | | | | | | | |
| *The Legend of Sleepy Hollow* | | | | | | | | | |
| *King Midas and the Golden Touch* | | | | | | | | | |

The Unexpected

# Fluency Graph

Name: _____  Class: _____

**WCPM RATE** — Number of words read correctly in one minute

1. Read a fluency passage for one minute.
2. Find the next open column.
3. Color the column to the number that shows how far you read.
4. Mark the number of errors in the chart at the bottom.

ERRORS — Above 6

The Unexpected

# Book Summaries

## Making Gold
### By Ilie Ruby

**Summary**

When mysterious advertisements fall from the sky, many people in a poor neighborhood respond by sending for a machine they can use to make gold. The machine costs just 25 dollars and seven good deeds a day. Sam and Pam are not fooled by the ads. They set out to find the mysterious Mr. Rich and reveal his scheme. Pam and Sam solve the mystery but find they have been wrong about Mr. Rich's motives. The scheme brings the neighborhood something that is far more valuable than gold.

**Literary Terms**

**Suspense:** arousing the reader's curiosity or making the reader wonder what will happen next

**Plot:** sequence of events with rising action, conflict, climax, and resolution

**Other Resources**

**Book:** Engel, Peter H. *Scam: Shams, Stings, and Shady Business Practices and How You Can Avoid Them* (St. Martin's, 1996)

**Movies:** *Alchemy—Science of Magic* (2000)

**Web sites:** http://www.fraudaid.com
http://www.levity.com/alchemy

## Born Dead: The Story of Gordon Parks
### By Barbara Wood

**Summary**

Gordon Parks did not have an easy start in life. Parks was one of 15 children in a poor African American family. When he was born, everyone thought he was dead. But Parks came to life with a vengeance. Through hard work and the wise use of his many talents, Parks made a name for himself by taking photographs, authoring books, and making movies. Parks knew how to teach and entertain at the same time. He continued to use his talents and experiences to be a warrior in the battle against racism.

**Literary Term**

**Biography:** an account of a person's life written by another person

**Other Resources**

**Book:** Parks, Gordon. *The Learning Tree* (Fawcett Crest Books, 1976)

**Movie:** *The Learning Tree* (1969)

**Web site:** http://www.tfaoi.com/newsm1/n1m673.htm

## The Navel of the World
### By Catherine Podojil

**Summary**

Easter Island is a mysterious place dotted with enormous statues that were carved long ago. Because most of the history of Easter Island has been lost, no one is sure just who carved the statues, why they were carved, or how the heavy statues were moved to their permanent locations. The native people called Easter Island the "navel of the world" because to them it was the center of the universe. Readers learn modern theories about the people and statues on the island.

**Literary Term**

**Nonfiction:** a factual piece of literature

**Other Resources**

**Books:** Arnold, Caroline. *Easter Island: Giant Stone Statues Tell of a Rich and Tragic Past* (Houghton-Mifflin, 2000); Orliac, Catherine, et al. *Easter Island: Mystery of the Stone Giants* (Harry N. Abrams, 1995)

**Web site:** http://www.pbs.org/wgbh/nova/easter/

## The Mountain Is on Fire!
### By Carole Gerber

**Summary**

In A.D. 79, an erupting volcano destroyed the ancient city of Pompeii and many of its people. In 1980 another volcano, Mount St. Helens in the state of Washington, became known for the destruction it caused and the lives it took. By that time, however, scientists understood why volcanoes erupt. They were able to predict when Mount St. Helens would explode. Readers learn the how and why of volcanoes and how scientists' warnings save lives today.

**Literary Term**

**Nonfiction:** a factual piece of literature

**Other Resources**

**Books:** Amery, Colin and Brian Curran, Jr. *The Lost World of Pompeii* (J. Paul Getty Trust Publications, 2002); Carson, Rob. *Mount St. Helens: The Eruption and Recovery of a Volcano* (Sasquatch Books, 2000)

**Web site:** http://www.learner.org/exhibits/volcanoes/forecast.html

# Book Summaries

## Atlantis: Land of Mystery
### By Linda Lott

**Summary**
Ana's grandfather tells her the story of Atlantis, a perfect place that sank into the sea many years ago. But how much of the story is true? Readers learn the origin of the legend of Atlantis along with some theories about whether Atlantis really existed, where Atlantis might have been located, and what may have happened to the people who lived there.

**Literary Terms**
**Fiction:** a piece of literature that is invented
**Legend:** a popular story, usually treated as historical fact but not verifiable

**Other Resources**
**Books:** McMullen, David. *Atlantis: The Missing Continent* (Steck-Vaughn, 1992); Wallace, Holly. *The Mystery of Atlantis* (Heinemann Library, 1999)

**Movies:** *Atlantis: The Lost Empire* (2001); *Lost City of Atlantis* (1978)

**Web site:** http://www.activemind.com/Mysterious/Topics/Atlantis

## Master of Disaster
### By Nick Pease

**Summary:**
Natural disasters happen everywhere, and it is important to be prepared. This book highlights several types of natural disasters: tornadoes, extreme heat and cold, hurricanes, tsunamis, and earthquakes. Some well-known examples of these disasters are discussed, and the forces that cause them are explained. In addition, the author provides simple, practical safety suggestions for coping with each type of disaster.

**Literary Term**
**Nonfiction:** a factual piece of literature

**Other Resources**
**Books:** Simon, Seymour. *Tornadoes* (HarperCollins, 1999); Wiesner, David. *Hurricane* (Clarion Books; Reprint edition, 1992)

**Web site:** http://www.fema.gov/kids/tch_bks.htm

## The Legend of Sleepy Hollow
### Retold by Rick Watson

**Summary**
Tall, lanky Ichabod Crane comes to Sleepy Hollow as the new schoolmaster and makes an enemy when he plans to marry Katrina. Brom Bones, the local bully, already has his eye on Katrina. Annoyed by the competition, Brom uses Ichabod's fear and an old tale about a neighborhood ghost called the Headless Horseman to take revenge on Ichabod and to win Katrina for himself.

**Author**
Washington Irving was born in 1783 and lived most of his life on the banks of the Hudson River, where this story takes place. Another of Irving's well-known stories is *Rip Van Winkle*.

**Literary Terms**
**Foreshadowing:** an author's hints about events that will occur later in the story
**Legend:** a popular story, usually treated as historical fact but not verifiable
**Setting:** the story environment; its time and place

**Other Resources**
**Movies:** *The Legend of Sleepy Hollow* (1979, 1988); *Sleepy Hollow* (1999)

**Web site:** http://www. online-literature.com/irving/geoffrey_crayon

## King Midas and the Golden Touch
### By Carole Gerber

**Summary**
King Midas has lots of gold but wants more. He is thrilled when a god grants his wish to have everything he touches turn to gold. At first, things go well for Midas. He runs through the palace grounds, turning everything to gold. Then Midas learns his wish has a bad side. Food and water turn to gold before he can eat or drink. Golden roses have no scent. Worst of all, the person Midas loves most, his daughter, turns into a golden statue when she touches him. Midas learns there are more important things than gold, and is relieved when the god agrees to take away the golden touch.

**Literary Terms**
**Moral:** the lesson a story teaches or implies
**Myth:** story from long ago or another culture that involves superhuman beings or gods

**Other Resources**
**Books:** *D'Aulaires' Book of Greek Myths* (A Doubleday Book for Young Readers, 1962); Storr, Catherine. *King Midas* (Raintree Children's Books, 1985)

**Web sites:** http://www.mythweb.com
http://www.bulfinch.org/fables/welcome.html

The Unexpected

# Building Background

Name _____ Date _____

## *Making Gold*
## What You Know

**Write answers to these questions.**

1. Find out what gold is, where it comes from, and if it can be made. Write your answers on a separate sheet of paper.

2. What are some good deeds that students in your school do for the community?

   _____

   _____

3. If you could make one improvement to your school or community, what would it be?

   _____

   _____

## Word Meanings
### *Definitions*

**Look for these words as you read your chapter book. When you find one of these words, write its definition.**

allergic: _____

instructions: _____

junkyard: _____

machine: _____

neighbors: _____

chef: _____

# Word Lists

## *Making Gold*

| | Unfamiliar Words | Word Meanings | Proper Nouns | |
|---|---|---|---|---|
| | knew<br>poor<br>sky<br>whole | neighbors | Aunt Jo | Chapter 1 |
| | collecting<br>empty<br>flew<br>phone<br>porch<br>signed<br>spy<br>though<br>waste | machine | Hornet<br>Pam Wu<br>Tyrone | Chapter 2 |
| | fries<br>invited<br>object<br>sprinkle<br>world | instructions | Dobbs<br>French<br>Mr. Santos<br>Saturday | Chapter 3 |
| | bottle<br>center<br>tied | | Loafer | Chapter 4 |
| | music<br>toward<br>visit<br>wedding | allergic<br>chef | China<br>Mrs. Jackson | Chapter 5 |
| | build<br>crowd<br>fingerprints<br>forward<br>promise<br>stranger<br>sugar<br>touched | junkyard | Mr. Gibb | Chapter 6 |

The Unexpected • Book 1

# Chapter Quiz

Name _____  Date _____

## *Making Gold*
## Chapter 1, "Hard Times"

**Mark each statement *T* for true or *F* for false.**

____ 1. Sam's family was poor.

____ 2. Sam thought his mother worked too hard.

____ 3. Sam wanted to get a big house for his mother.

____ 4. Sam had to stay on his side of the street.

____ 5. People on the other side of the street were rich.

____ 6. Sam hated being poor.

____ 7. Sam was not allowed to play football.

____ 8. Sam's aunt lived with them.

____ 9. Sam's mother worked at a store.

____ 10. Sam is telling this story.

**Read the question, and write your answer.**

Why is this chapter called "Hard Times"?

_____

_____

# Chapter Quiz

Name _____ Date _____

## *Making Gold*
### Chapter 2, "Get Rich!"

**Fill in the bubble beside the answer for each question.**

1. What did Sam call himself?
    - Ⓐ the Hornet
    - Ⓑ the Bear
    - Ⓒ the Bee

2. What hit Sam on the head?
    - Ⓐ a bird
    - Ⓑ a football
    - Ⓒ a paper airplane

3. The paper airplane was really
    - Ⓐ 25 dollars.
    - Ⓑ a gold machine.
    - Ⓒ an ad.

4. What was on the airplane's wings?
    - Ⓐ gold dust
    - Ⓑ money
    - Ⓒ feathers

**Read the question, and write your answer.**

What do you think will happen in the next chapter? _____
_____
_____

The Unexpected • Book 1

# Chapter Quiz

Name _____ Date _____

## *Making Gold*
### Chapter 3, "The Gold Machine"

**Number the events in order from 1 to 5.**

___ Sam's mother found an airplane on her car.

___ Mr. Santos waved to Sam.

___ There was a new football for Sam on the porch.

___ Sam took off on his bike.

___ There was a gold machine on every porch.

**Number the events in order from 6 to 10.**

___ "On Saturday you will get a box of gold dust."

___ "Bake the object in the machine."

___ Aunt Jo was reading the gold machine's instructions.

___ "Let the gold cool for ten minutes."

___ "Sprinkle it on any object."

**Read the question, and write your answer.**

Do you think the gold machine will work? Why or why not?

_____

_____

**Chapter Quiz**

Name _____ Date _____

## *Making Gold*
### Chapter 4, "Seven Good Deeds"

**Fill in the bubble beside the answer for each question.**

1. How did Mr. Santos feel about doing good deeds?
   - Ⓐ It made him happy.
   - Ⓑ It made him tired.
   - Ⓒ He did not care.

2. What did Sam's mother help plan?
   - Ⓐ a car wash
   - Ⓑ a neighborhood center
   - Ⓒ a football game

3. Why did people do more than seven good deeds?
   - Ⓐ They had to.
   - Ⓑ They wanted to.
   - Ⓒ Mr. Rich said to.

4. Who gave Sam the new football?
   - Ⓐ his mother
   - Ⓑ Mr. Rich
   - Ⓒ Pam Wu

**Read the question, and write your answer.**

What do you think will happen in the next chapter? _____
_____
_____

The Unexpected • Book 1

# Chapter Quiz

Name _____ Date _____

## *Making Gold*
### Chapter 5, "The Chase"

**Mark each statement *T* for true or *F* for false.**

___ 1. People were in the street because they were mad.

___ 2. Mrs. Wu used to be a chef in China.

___ 3. Tin Man poked Sam.

___ 4. Pam thinks "Mr. Rich" is really a woman.

___ 5. Summer school was still going on when Sam and Pam got there.

___ 6. Mrs. Jackson was in her car.

___ 7. Mrs. Jackson was waiting under a tree.

___ 8. Pam thought Mrs. Jackson was Mr. Rich.

___ 9. Mrs. Jackson loves to wear gold jewelry.

___ 10. Mrs. Jackson could not be Mr. Rich.

**Read the question, and write your answer.**

Why does Pam think Mrs. Jackson is Mr. Rich? _____

_____

# Chapter Quiz

Name _____  Date _____

## *Making Gold*
### Chapter 6, "The Richest Street"

**Number the events in order from 1 to 5.**

____ Sam's mother wanted to bake a cake to cheer them up.

____ Sam tried to pay for the sugar, but Mr. Gibb gave the money back to him.

____ Sam saw gold on the dollar bills.

____ Sam went to the store to buy sugar.

____ There were no boxes of gold dust.

**Number the events in order from 6 to 10.**

____ Dobbs said the money was for a neighborhood center.

____ Sam and Pam rode to the junkyard and found the gold van.

____ The neighborhood center was built.

____ Mr. Gibb said the gold paint on the bills came from Dobbs.

____ A crowd formed around Dobbs's house.

**Read the question, and write your answer.**

Why did Dobbs trick the people in the neighborhood? Do you think what he did was right? Explain your answer.

_____

_____

_____

The Unexpected • Book 1

# Thinking and Writing

Name _____ Date _____

## *Making Gold*
### Think About It

**Write about or give an oral presentation for each question.**

1. Do you think Dobbs was a crook? Why or why not?

   _____
   _____

2. Suspense means not knowing what will happen next. Give examples of suspense from the book.

   _____
   _____

3. Aunt Jo said Sam and his mother were dreamers. Why is it good to be a dreamer? What is bad about being a dreamer?

   _____
   _____

4. How could you help make your neighborhood better?

   _____
   _____

## Write About It

**Choose one of the questions below. Write your answer on a sheet of paper.**

1. Write about the new neighborhood center. What is it called? What does it look like? What does it have inside? Give details so your readers can picture it.

2. Sam and Pam made a good team. They solved the mystery. Make up a new mystery story. Use Sam and Pam as the main characters.

3. Complete the Story Grammar Map for this book.

# Fluency Passages

## *Making Gold*

**Chapter 1** *pages 1 and 2*

| | |
|---|---|
| *On summer nights I would sit on the steps and talk to the neighbors | 14 |
| on my side of the street. And I had to stay on my side of the street. "They" | 32 |
| lived on the other side of the street. No one knew why they didn't like | 47 |
| us—or why we didn't like them. It had just always been that way. | 61 |
| We were poor. The people on the other side of the street were poor. | 75 |
| No big deal, right? | 79 |
| It really didn't matter much to me. I went to school.* And I played | 93 |
| football. Nothing could stop me from playing football. | 101 |

**Chapter 6** *pages 24 and 25*

| | |
|---|---|
| *"Why did you do it, Mr. Rich?" I asked. | 9 |
| Mr. Gibb looked at the bills. | 15 |
| "I didn't do it," he said. He showed me his new sign out front. Dobbs | 30 |
| had just dropped it off. | 35 |
| "See? The gold leaf is still wet," Mr. Gibb said. | 45 |
| "Gold what?" I asked. | 49 |
| "Paint. It's made from real gold." | 55 |
| My head was spinning. Could Dobbs be Mr. Rich? No. He drives a | 68 |
| blue truck, not a gold van. I had seen the truck parked by his house near | 84 |
| the junkyard. | 86 |
| I went home and* dropped off the sugar. Then I met Pam. We rode | 100 |
| our bikes to the junkyard. | 105 |

---

- The target rate for **The Unexpected** is 90 wcpm. The asterisks (*) mark 90 words.
- Listen to the student read the passage. Count the number of words read in one minute and the number of errors.
- For the reading rate, subtract the number of errors from the total number of words read.
- Have students enter their scores on their **Fluency Graph.** See page 9.

The Unexpected • Book 1

# Answer Key

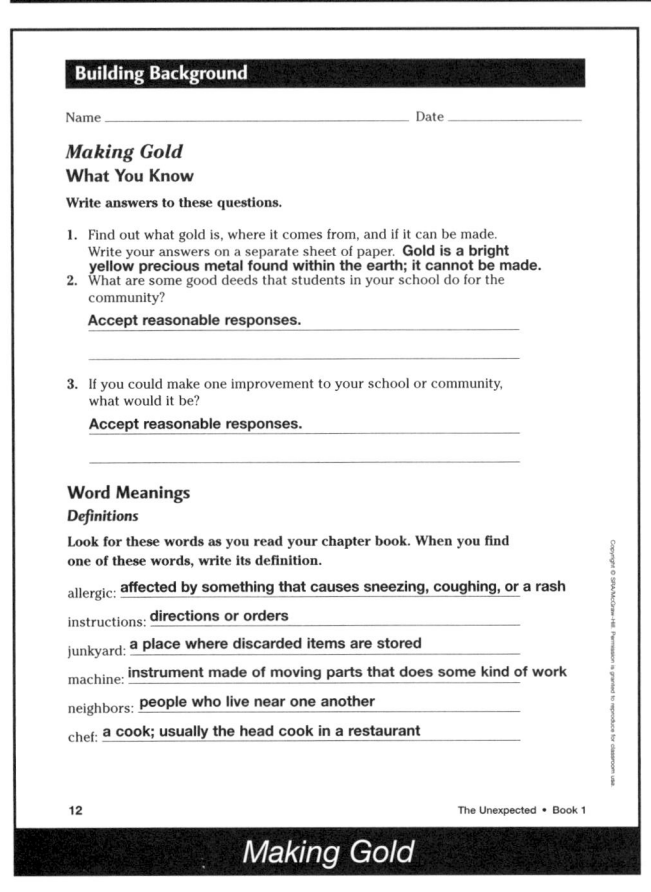

## Building Background

Name _____ Date _____

*Making Gold*
**What You Know**
Write answers to these questions.

1. Find out what gold is, where it comes from, and if it can be made. Write your answers on a separate sheet of paper. **Gold is a bright yellow precious metal found within the earth; it cannot be made.**
2. What are some good deeds that students in your school do for the community?
   **Accept reasonable responses.**

3. If you could make one improvement to your school or community, what would it be?
   **Accept reasonable responses.**

**Word Meanings**
*Definitions*
Look for these words as you read your chapter book. When you find one of these words, write its definition.

allergic: **affected by something that causes sneezing, coughing, or a rash**
instructions: **directions or orders**
junkyard: **a place where discarded items are stored**
machine: **instrument made of moving parts that does some kind of work**
neighbors: **people who live near one another**
chef: **a cook; usually the head cook in a restaurant**

12

---

## Chapter Quiz

Name _____ Date _____

*Making Gold*
**Chapter 1, "Hard Times"**
Mark each statement *T* for true or *F* for false.

__T__ 1. Sam's family was poor.
__T__ 2. Sam thought his mother worked too hard.
__T__ 3. Sam wanted to get a big house for his mother.
__T__ 4. Sam had to stay on his side of the street.
__F__ 5. People on the other side of the street were rich.
__F__ 6. Sam hated being poor.
__F__ 7. Sam was not allowed to play football.
__T__ 8. Sam's aunt lived with them.
__F__ 9. Sam's mother worked at a store.
__T__ 10. Sam is telling this story.

Read the question, and write your answer.
Why is this chapter called "Hard Times"?
**Ideas: People are poor; mother works too hard; times are hard for everyone on the street.**

14

---

## Chapter Quiz

Name _____ Date _____

*Making Gold*
**Chapter 2, "Get Rich!"**
Fill in the bubble beside the answer for each question.

1. What did Sam call himself?
   ● the Hornet
   Ⓑ the Bear
   Ⓒ the Bee

2. What hit Sam on the head?
   Ⓐ a bird
   Ⓑ a football
   ● a paper airplane

3. The paper airplane was really
   Ⓐ 25 dollars.
   Ⓑ a gold machine.
   ● an ad.

4. What was on the airplane's wings?
   ● gold dust
   Ⓑ money
   Ⓒ feathers

Read the question, and write your answer.
What do you think will happen in the next chapter? **Accept reasonable responses.**

15

---

## Chapter Quiz

Name _____ Date _____

*Making Gold*
**Chapter 3, "The Gold Machine"**
Number the events in order from 1 to 5.

__5__ Sam's mother found an airplane on her car.
__3__ Mr. Santos waved to Sam.
__4__ There was a new football for Sam on the porch.
__2__ Sam took off on his bike.
__1__ There was a gold machine on every porch.

Number the events in order from 6 to 10.

__7__ "On Saturday you will get a box of gold dust."
__9__ "Bake the object in the machine."
__6__ Aunt Jo was reading the gold machine's instructions.
__10__ "Let the gold cool for ten minutes."
__8__ "Sprinkle it on any object."

Read the question, and write your answer.
Do you think the gold machine will work? Why or why not?
**Answers will vary.**

16

---

22     The Unexpected • Book 1

# Answer Key

## Chapter Quiz

Name _____ Date _____

*Making Gold*
**Chapter 4, "Seven Good Deeds"**

**Fill in the bubble beside the answer for each question.**

1. How did Mr. Santos feel about doing good deeds?
   - ● It made him happy.
   - Ⓑ It made him tired.
   - Ⓒ He did not care.

2. What did Sam's mother help plan?
   - Ⓐ a car wash
   - ● a neighborhood center
   - Ⓒ a football game

3. Why did people do more than seven good deeds?
   - Ⓐ They had to.
   - ● They wanted to.
   - Ⓒ Mr. Rich said to.

4. Who gave Sam the new football?
   - Ⓐ his mother
   - Ⓑ Mr. Rich
   - ● Pam Wu

**Read the question, and write your answer.**

What do you think will happen in the next chapter? **Accept reasonable responses.**

*Making Gold* — page 17

## Chapter Quiz

Name _____ Date _____

*Making Gold*
**Chapter 5, "The Chase"**

**Mark each statement *T* for true or *F* for false.**

- **F** 1. People were in the street because they were mad.
- **T** 2. Mrs. Wu used to be a chef in China.
- **F** 3. Tin Man poked Sam.
- **T** 4. Pam thinks "Mr. Rich" is really a woman.
- **F** 5. Summer school was still going on when Sam and Pam got there.
- **F** 6. Mrs. Jackson was in her car.
- **T** 7. Mrs. Jackson was waiting under a tree.
- **T** 8. Pam thought Mrs. Jackson was Mr. Rich.
- **F** 9. Mrs. Jackson loves to wear gold jewelry.
- **T** 10. Mrs. Jackson could not be Mr. Rich.

**Read the question, and write your answer.**

Why does Pam think Mrs. Jackson is Mr. Rich? **Mrs. Jackson drives a gold van.**

*Making Gold* — page 18

## Chapter Quiz

Name _____ Date _____

*Making Gold*
**Chapter 6, "The Richest Street"**

**Number the events in order from 1 to 5.**

- **2** Sam's mother wanted to bake a cake to cheer them up.
- **4** Sam tried to pay for the sugar, but Mr. Gibb gave the money back to him.
- **5** Sam saw gold on the dollar bills.
- **3** Sam went to the store to buy sugar.
- **1** There were no boxes of gold dust.

**Number the events in order from 6 to 10.**

- **9** Dobbs said the money was for a neighborhood center.
- **7** Sam and Pam rode to the junkyard and found the gold van.
- **10** The neighborhood center was built.
- **6** Mr. Gibb said the gold paint on the bills came from Dobbs.
- **8** A crowd formed around Dobbs's house.

**Read the question, and write your answer.**

Why did Dobbs trick the people in the neighborhood? Do you think what he did was right? Explain your answer.
**Answers will vary.**

*Making Gold* — page 19

## Thinking and Writing

Name _____ Date _____

*Making Gold*
**Think About It**

**Write about or give an oral presentation for each question.**

1. Do you think Dobbs was a crook? Why or why not?
   **Idea: He was not a crook because he did not keep the money and did a good deed.**

2. Suspense means not knowing what will happen next. Give examples of suspense from the book.
   **Ideas: Who was Mr. Rich? How did the machine work? Why did they have to do good deeds?**

3. Aunt Jo said Sam and his mother were dreamers. Why is it good to be a dreamer? What is bad about being a dreamer?
   **Ideas: Dreaming helps set goals; without action, dreaming can be a waste of time.**

4. How could you help make your neighborhood better?
   **Ideas: clean it up; make it friendlier, safer, or brighter at night**

**Write About It**

**Choose one of the questions below. Write your answer on a sheet of paper.**

1. Write about the new neighborhood center. What is it called? What does it look like? What does it have inside? Give details so your readers can picture it.

2. Sam and Pam made a good team. They solved the mystery. Make up a new mystery story. Use Sam and Pam as the main characters.

3. Complete the Story Grammar Map for this book.

*Making Gold* — page 20

The Unexpected • Book 1     23

# Building Background

Name _____ Date _____

## *Born Dead: The Story of Gordon Parks*
### What You Know

**Write answers to these questions.**

1. Why might some people treat others differently because of their race?

   _____

   _____

2. What is a biography? How does it differ from an autobiography?

   _____

   _____

3. Why do people take photographs? _____

   _____

4. If you were going to photograph a historical event, what kinds of photos would you take? _____

   _____

## Word Meanings
### Matching

**Look for these words as you read your chapter book. When you find a word, draw a line to connect the word with the correct definition.**

| | |
|---|---|
| fashion | words written in verse that create an emotional response |
| photograph | a person who plays the piano |
| pianist | treating people differently because of the color of their skin |
| poetry | stylish clothing |
| racism | something used in a fight or battle |
| weapon | a picture taken by a camera |

# Word Lists

## Born Dead: The Story of Gordon Parks

| Unfamiliar Words | Word Meanings | Proper Nouns | |
|---|---|---|---|
| dead, movie, poor, since, unfair | photograph | African American, Fort Scott, Gordon Parks, Kansas | Chapter 1 |
| bandleader, child, color, concert, differently, learn, library, music, number, piano, poem, radio, taught, wrote | pianist, racism | Caucasian, Minnesota | Chapter 2 |
| against, camera, change, choice, civil, farmworkers, gained, government, knew, magazine, movement, museums, offered, place, poverty | fashion, weapon | Harlem, Washington, D.C. | Chapter 3 |
| paid, starve, world | | Brazil, Flavio da Silva, Rio de Janeiro, United States | Chapter 4 |
| destroy, faced, fight, novel, painting, title, total, young | poetry | *A Choice of Weapons*, *The Learning Tree* | Chapter 5 |
| award, friend, instead | | | Chapter 6 |

The Unexpected • Book 2

# Chapter Quiz

Name _____ Date _____

## *Born Dead: The Story of Gordon Parks*
## Chapter 1, "Hollering"

**Mark each statement *T* for true or *F* for false.**

_____ 1. At first the baby boy seemed to be dead.

_____ 2. The baby was dunked in warm water.

_____ 3. Cold water made the baby holler.

_____ 4. Gordon Parks was born in 1712.

_____ 5. Parks was born in New York City.

_____ 6. *Holler* means "yell or shout."

_____ 7. Parks wanted people to hear his ideas.

_____ 8. Parks wrote books and poetry.

_____ 9. All Parks's photographs show sad things.

_____ 10. Parks made movies and wrote songs.

**Read the question, and write your answer.**

How did Parks tell people about African American life? _____

_____

_____

# Chapter Quiz

Name _____ Date _____

## *Born Dead: The Story of Gordon Parks*
### Chapter 2, "Hard Times"

**Fill in the bubble beside the answer for each question.**

1. Why was life hard for Parks?
   - Ⓐ He was African American.
   - Ⓑ He was poor.
   - Ⓒ both A and B

2. What did Parks's mother do for him?
   - Ⓐ helped him feel good about himself
   - Ⓑ sent him to college
   - Ⓒ bought his first camera

3. What did Parks's mother tell him to do?
   - Ⓐ take photos
   - Ⓑ treat others well
   - Ⓒ play baseball

4. Parks worked at a club. There he
   - Ⓐ learned to play the piano.
   - Ⓑ read books in the library.
   - Ⓒ learned to cook.

**Read the question, and write your answer.**

What role did music play in Parks's work? _____
_____
_____

The Unexpected • Book 2

# Chapter Quiz

Name _____ Date _____

## *Born Dead: The Story of Gordon Parks*
### Chapter 3, "Fighting with Photos"

**Fill in the bubble beside the answer for each question.**

1. How did Parks learn to take photos?
   - Ⓐ by going to museums
   - Ⓑ by reading books
   - Ⓒ both A and B

2. What became Parks's weapon against poverty and racism?
   - Ⓐ money and fame
   - Ⓑ a gang
   - Ⓒ the camera

3. What did Parks find in Washington, D.C.?
   - Ⓐ less racism than in Kansas
   - Ⓑ more racism than in Kansas
   - Ⓒ no racism

4. What did Parks's photos help people do?
   - Ⓐ forget about people
   - Ⓑ see the truth about life
   - Ⓒ forget about racism

**Read the question, and write your answer.**

Why did Parks take photographs of African Americans? _____

_____

# Chapter Quiz

Name _____ Date _____

## *Born Dead: The Story of Gordon Parks*
### Chapter 4, "Flavio's Story"

**Number the events in order from 1 to 5.**

____ Parks took photos of Flavio da Silva.

____ Parks went to Brazil.

____ *Life* magazine told da Silva's story.

____ Parks met da Silva.

____ *Life* sent Parks all over the world.

**Number the events in order from 6 to 10.**

____ Da Silva came to the United States.

____ Da Silva's family found a better place to live.

____ People read about da Silva in *Life*.

____ Doctors helped da Silva get well.

____ People sent money to help da Silva.

**Read the question, and write your answer.**

Why did Parks take pictures of da Silva? _____

_____

_____

# Chapter Quiz

Name _____ Date _____

## *Born Dead: The Story of Gordon Parks*
### Chapter 5, "Writing"

**Mark each statement *T* for true or *F* for false.**

____ 1. Parks did not like to write.

____ 2. Parks wrote a poetry book first.

____ 3. Parks's mom called Kansas his "learning tree."

____ 4. Parks wrote a book called *The Learning Tree*.

____ 5. Few people read *The Learning Tree*.

____ 6. *A Choice of Weapons* is about Parks's life after his mother died.

____ 7. Parks wrote just about sad things.

____ 8. Parks never wrote about love and hope.

____ 9. Parks never stopped trying new things.

____ 10. He told stories with photos, words, and paintings.

**Read the question, and write your answer.**

What did Parks write about in his poems? _____

_____

_____

**Chapter Quiz**

Name _____ Date _____

# *Born Dead: The Story of Gordon Parks*
## Chapter 6, "Ready to Start"

**Fill in the bubble beside the answer for each question.**

1. What talents did Parks have?
   - Ⓐ taking photos and painting
   - Ⓑ playing the piano and writing books
   - Ⓒ both A and B

2. What was the name of Parks's first movie?
   - Ⓐ *The Learning Tree*
   - Ⓑ *Flavio*
   - Ⓒ *No Love*

3. What happened after da Silva's story was in *Life*?
   - Ⓐ Parks and da Silva stayed friends.
   - Ⓑ Da Silva did not like Parks anymore.
   - Ⓒ Parks forgot about da Silva.

4. How old was Parks when he said, "I'm just ready to start"?
   - Ⓐ 45
   - Ⓑ 65
   - Ⓒ 85

**Read the question, and write your answer.**

How did Parks help other African Americans, and why was he considered a role model? _____

_____

_____

The Unexpected • Book 2

# Thinking and Writing

Name _____ Date _____

## *Born Dead: The Story of Gordon Parks*
## Think About It

**Write about or give an oral presentation for each question.**

1. What things helped make Parks the man he was? _____
   _____
   _____

2. How can a camera be a weapon? What did Parks fight against with his camera? _____
   _____
   _____

3. How did Parks help people see things that should be changed?
   _____
   _____

## Write About It

**Choose one of the questions below. Write your answer on a sheet of paper.**

1. Parks liked poetry. Write a poem about him.

2. Think about this sentence: "Parks liked to try new things." Write a paragraph that starts with this sentence. Use things you learned about Parks from the story to write this paragraph.

3. Some people say, "A picture is worth a thousand words." Do you agree? Do you think Parks agreed? Why or why not?

4. Complete the Sequencing Chart for this book.

# Fluency Passages

## *Born Dead: The Story of Gordon Parks*

**Chapter 2** *pages 6 and 7*

| | |
|---|---:|
| *The club had a library. Parks had quit school when his mom died. | 13 |
| But he didn't stop learning. He read everything he could. He learned a lot | 27 |
| from books. | 29 |
| Soon Parks needed to find a new job. Once again he started playing | 42 |
| the piano. Many people began calling him "Blue" because he always | 53 |
| played the blues. | 56 |
| Parks wanted to write music. But he didn't know how to write it on a | 71 |
| music scale. So he made up his own way. He gave each note a number. | 86 |
| Then he wrote his* songs using those numbers. | 94 |
| "No Love" was the first hit song he wrote. | 103 |

**Chapter 4** *page 19*

| | |
|---|---:|
| *Parks took many photos of the boy. The photos showed the truth | 12 |
| about being poor. *Life* magazine used Parks's photos to tell da Silva's | 24 |
| story. | 25 |
| People read the story and looked at the photos. They learned about | 37 |
| da Silva. No one wanted him to die. | 45 |
| Many people wanted to help. They sent da Silva letters. They sent | 57 |
| him money. Best of all, some doctors read the story. They wanted to help | 71 |
| da Silva get well. | 75 |
| So da Silva came to the United States. The money people had sent | 88 |
| him paid* for the trip. The doctors helped him get well. | 99 |

---

- The target rate for **The Unexpected** is 90 wcpm. The asterisks (*) mark 90 words.
- Listen to the student read the passage. Count the number of words read in one minute and the number of errors.
- For the reading rate, subtract the number of errors from the total number of words read.
- Have students enter their scores on their **Fluency Graph.** See page 9.

# Answer Key

## Building Background

Name _____ Date _____

*Born Dead: The Story of Gordon Parks*
**What You Know**
Write answers to these questions.

1. Why might some people treat others differently because of their race?
   **Accept reasonable responses.**

2. What is a biography? How does it differ from an autobiography?
   **A biography is a history of a person's life; an autobiography is the story of a person's life written by that same person.**

3. Why do people take photographs? **Ideas: to remember an event or people; to create visual memories**

4. If you were going to photograph a historical event, what kinds of photos would you take? **Accept reasonable responses.**

**Word Meanings**
*Matching*

Look for these words as you read your chapter book. When you find a word, draw a line to connect the word with the correct definition.

- fashion — stylish clothing
- photograph — a picture taken by a camera
- pianist — a person who plays the piano
- poetry — words written in verse that create an emotional response
- racism — treating people differently because of the color of their skin
- weapon — something used in a fight or battle

---

## Chapter Quiz

Name _____ Date _____

*Born Dead: The Story of Gordon Parks*
Chapter 1, "Hollering"
Mark each statement *T* for true or *F* for false.

- **T** 1. At first the baby boy seemed to be dead.
- **F** 2. The baby was dunked in warm water.
- **T** 3. Cold water made the baby holler.
- **F** 4. Gordon Parks was born in 1712.
- **F** 5. Parks was born in New York City.
- **T** 6. *Holler* means "yell or shout."
- **T** 7. Parks wanted people to hear his ideas.
- **T** 8. Parks wrote books and poetry.
- **F** 9. All Parks's photographs show sad things.
- **T** 10. Parks made movies and wrote songs.

Read the question, and write your answer.

How did Parks tell people about African American life?
**with movies, songs, words, and photographs**

---

## Chapter Quiz

Name _____ Date _____

*Born Dead: The Story of Gordon Parks*
Chapter 2, "Hard Times"
Fill in the bubble beside the answer for each question.

1. Why was life hard for Parks?
   - Ⓐ He was African American.
   - Ⓑ He was poor.
   - ● both A and B

2. What did Parks's mother do for him?
   - ● helped him feel good about himself
   - Ⓑ sent him to college
   - Ⓒ bought his first camera

3. What did Parks's mother tell him to do?
   - Ⓐ take photos
   - ● treat others well
   - Ⓒ play baseball

4. Parks worked at a club. There he
   - Ⓐ learned to play the piano.
   - ● read books in the library.
   - Ⓒ learned to cook.

Read the question, and write your answer.

What role did music play in Parks's work? **Ideas: wrote songs; heard music in his poems; saw music in his photos; wrote the music for his movies**

---

## Chapter Quiz

Name _____ Date _____

*Born Dead: The Story of Gordon Parks*
Chapter 3, "Fighting with Photos"
Fill in the bubble beside the answer for each question.

1. How did Parks learn to take photos?
   - Ⓐ by going to museums
   - Ⓑ by reading books
   - ● both A and B

2. What became Parks's weapon against poverty and racism?
   - Ⓐ money and fame
   - Ⓑ a gang
   - ● the camera

3. What did Parks find in Washington, D.C.?
   - Ⓐ less racism than in Kansas
   - ● more racism than in Kansas
   - Ⓒ no racism

4. What did Parks's photos help people do?
   - Ⓐ forget about people
   - ● see the truth about life
   - Ⓒ forget about racism

Read the question, and write your answer.

Why did Parks take photographs of African Americans?
**Idea: wanted people to know how hard life was for African Americans, to see the problems African Americans faced**

# Answer Key

## Chapter Quiz

Name _____ Date _____

*Born Dead: The Story of Gordon Parks*
**Chapter 4, "Flavio's Story"**

**Number the events in order from 1 to 5.**

_4_ Parks took photos of Flavio da Silva.
_2_ Parks went to Brazil.
_5_ *Life* magazine told da Silva's story.
_3_ Parks met da Silva.
_1_ *Life* sent Parks all over the world.

**Number the events in order from 6 to 10.**

_8_ Da Silva came to the United States.
_10_ Da Silva's family found a better place to live.
_6_ People read about da Silva in *Life*.
_9_ Doctors helped da Silva get well.
_7_ People sent money to help da Silva.

**Read the question, and write your answer.**

Why did Parks take pictures of da Silva? **to tell the true story of poor people living in Rio de Janeiro**

---

## Chapter Quiz

Name _____ Date _____

*Born Dead: The Story of Gordon Parks*
**Chapter 5, "Writing"**

**Mark each statement *T* for true or *F* for false.**

_F_ 1. Parks did not like to write.
_F_ 2. Parks wrote a poetry book first.
_T_ 3. Parks's mom called Kansas his "learning tree."
_T_ 4. Parks wrote a book called *The Learning Tree*.
_F_ 5. Few people read *The Learning Tree*.
_T_ 6. *A Choice of Weapons* is about Parks's life after his mother died.
_F_ 7. Parks wrote just about sad things.
_F_ 8. Parks never wrote about love and hope.
_T_ 9. Parks never stopped trying new things.
_T_ 10. He told stories with photos, words, and paintings.

**Read the question, and write your answer.**

What did Parks write about in his poems? **racism, being poor, hope**

---

## Chapter Quiz

Name _____ Date _____

*Born Dead: The Story of Gordon Parks*
**Chapter 6, "Ready to Start"**

**Fill in the bubble beside the answer for each question.**

1. What talents did Parks have?
   Ⓐ taking photos and painting
   Ⓑ playing the piano and writing books
   ● both A and B

2. What was the name of Parks's first movie?
   Ⓐ *The Learning Tree*
   ● *Flavio*
   Ⓒ *No Love*

3. What happened after da Silva's story was in *Life*?
   ● Parks and da Silva stayed friends.
   Ⓑ Da Silva did not like Parks anymore.
   Ⓒ Parks forgot about da Silva.

4. How old was Parks when he said, "I'm just ready to start"?
   Ⓐ 45
   Ⓑ 65
   ● 85

**Read the question, and write your answer.**

How did Parks help other African Americans, and why was he considered a role model? **he brought attention to problems facing African Americans through photos, music, poetry, films; he opened the door for African Americans who wanted to make films**

---

## Thinking and Writing

Name _____ Date _____

*Born Dead: The Story of Gordon Parks*
**Think About It**

**Write about or give an oral presentation for each question.**

1. What things helped make Parks the man he was? **Ideas: his mother's love and lessons; growing up poor and African American; living on the streets; his determination and desire to learn new things**

2. How can a camera be a weapon? What did Parks fight against with his camera? **Ideas: Like other weapons, his camera was a tool for fighting; he used it to fight poverty and racism.**

3. How did Parks help people see things that should be changed? **Ideas: He used photos, poetry, books, music, films, paintings, and stories from his life.**

**Write About It**

**Choose one of the questions below. Write your answer on a sheet of paper.**

1. Parks liked poetry. Write a poem about him.
2. Think about this sentence: "Parks liked to try new things." Write a paragraph that starts with this sentence. Use things you learned about Parks from the story to write this paragraph.
3. Some people say, "A picture is worth a thousand words." Do you agree? Do you think Parks agreed? Why or why not?
4. Complete the Sequencing Chart for this book.

# Building Background

Name _____ Date _____

## *The Navel of the World*
## What You Know

**Write answers to these questions.**

1. What are some famous landmarks in the United States? Where are they located? Why are they famous? Write your answers on a separate sheet of paper.

2. Begin the What I Know/What I Learned Chart for this book. Complete the What I Know portion.

3. Why do you think artists create statues? _____
   _____

4. If you had to move something that weighed 20 or 30 tons, how would you do it? _____
   _____

5. What everyday tools make our lives much easier today?
   _____

## Word Meanings
### Definitions

**Look for these words as you read your chapter book. When you find one of these words, write its definition.**

aliens: _____

ancestors: _____

carve: _____

equinox: _____

navel: _____

statue: _____

# Word Lists

## *The Navel of the World*

| | Unfamiliar Words | Word Meanings | Proper Nouns |
|---|---|---|---|
| **Chapter 1** | grew<br>group<br>honor<br>might<br>*moai* [moh-AHee]<br>mysteries<br>place<br>settlers<br>soil<br>triangle<br>world | ancestors<br>carve<br>navel<br>statue | Easter Island<br>Polynesia<br>South Pacific<br>*Te Pito O Te Henua*<br>[te PEE-toh oh te<br>HAY-noo-ah] |
| **Chapter 2** | captain<br>destroyed<br>enough<br>forgotten<br>language<br>*rongorongo*<br>written | | Dutch<br>European<br>Peru |
| **Chapter 3** | *ahu* [AH-hoo]<br>colors<br>completed<br>crater<br>decorated<br>given<br>*pukao* [poo-KAH-oh]<br>volcano | | |
| **Chapter 4** | easily<br>legend<br>problem<br>prove<br>thought<br>tied<br>ton | | Thor Heyerdahl<br>[HAY-er-dahl] |
| **Chapter 5** | agree<br>brought<br>clue<br>mystery<br>potato<br>related<br>trace<br>true | | Pacific Ocean<br>*Rapa Nui*<br>[RAH-pah-NOO-e]<br>*Rapanui*<br>South America |
| **Chapter 6** | advanced<br>chiefs<br>during<br>earrings<br>face<br>known<br>nobles<br>reason<br>visit | aliens<br>equinox | *Ahu Akivi*<br>[AH-hoo ah-KEE-ree]<br>Atlantis |

The Unexpected • Book 3

# Chapter Quiz

Name _____  Date _____

## *The Navel of the World*
### Chapter 1, "The Navel of the World"

**Mark each statement *T* for true or *F* for false.**

____ 1. Easter Island has many stone statues.

____ 2. Scientists know who built the statues.

____ 3. Easter Island is small.

____ 4. Easter Island is in the Atlantic Ocean.

____ 5. The island is shaped like a circle.

____ 6. The closest land to Easter Island is 4,000 miles away.

____ 7. Easter Island was formed from three volcanoes.

____ 8. The island's first settlers were probably Polynesians.

____ 9. No plants grow on Easter Island.

____ 10. The island people thought Easter Island was the middle of the world.

**Read the question, and write your answer.**

Describe the geography of Easter Island. _____

_____

_____

**Chapter Quiz**

Name _____ Date _____

# *The Navel of the World*
## Chapter 2, "Easter Island"

**Fill in the bubble beside the answer for each question.**

1. Easter Island was named by
    - Ⓐ a Polynesian king.
    - Ⓑ a Dutch sea captain.
    - Ⓒ an island chief.

2. In the 1800s, people from Peru
    - Ⓐ built stone statues on the island.
    - Ⓑ built towns on the island.
    - Ⓒ took many of the islanders away.

3. Most of the statues, or *moai*,
    - Ⓐ were destroyed.
    - Ⓑ are still in good condition.
    - Ⓒ were stolen.

4. The language and history of the island
    - Ⓐ were kept in a safe place.
    - Ⓑ have been lost for a long time.
    - Ⓒ are known by people all over the world.

**Read the question, and write your answer.**

Why do we know so little about the history of Easter Island?

_____

_____

_____

The Unexpected • Book 3

# Chapter Quiz

Name _____ Date _____

## *The Navel of the World*
### Chapter 3, "Carving the Moai"

**Mark each statement *T* for true or *F* for false.**

____ 1. Soft rock from the volcanoes was good for carving.

____ 2. The carvers worked at the top of a mountain.

____ 3. The carvers started by drawing an outline on a rock wall.

____ 4. Moai could be carved very quickly.

____ 5. Carvers added stone eyes to the moai.

____ 6. Pukao look like earrings.

____ 7. Completed moai were moved to platforms.

____ 8. The islanders used ahu to move the moai across the island.

____ 9. There are still over 800 moai on Easter Island.

____ 10. Many moai still stand in the crater where they were made.

**Read the question, and write your answer.**

What was the purpose of the moai? How big are they?

_____

_____

_____

# Chapter Quiz

Name _____ Date _____

## *The Navel of the World*
### Chapter 4, "Moving the Moai"

**Number the events in order from 1 to 5.**

____ Islanders told Thor Heyerdahl the moai had been dragged across the island.

____ Ancient islanders moved the moai across the island.

____ Heyerdahl and his helpers made a sled from two logs.

____ In 1955 Heyerdahl went to Easter Island.

____ Heyerdahl decided to try to move a moai.

**Number the events in order from 6 to 10.**

____ The people moved a ten-ton moai.

____ Using ropes, Heyerdahl and his helpers lowered the statue onto the sled.

____ Using ropes tied to the sled, people pulled the sled with the moai.

____ Heyerdahl and his helpers tied ropes to the sled.

____ People tied ropes to a statue.

**Read the question, and write your answer.**

Why might some people believe that the moai walked?

_____

_____

_____

The Unexpected • Book 3

# Chapter Quiz

Name _____ Date _____

## *The Navel of the World*
### Chapter 5, "Who Made the Moai?"

**Mark each statement *T* for true or *F* for false.**

_____ 1. *Rapanui* is the term for the people and language of the island.

_____ 2. The Rapanui are not related to the early islanders.

_____ 3. The ancient islanders are still a mystery.

_____ 4. Sweet potatoes show that the first islanders might have come from Polynesia.

_____ 5. Heyerdahl tried to prove that Easter Islanders came from Peru.

_____ 6. Heyerdahl sailed on a modern sailboat.

_____ 7. Heyerdahl's boat drifted for many years.

_____ 8. Heyerdahl drifted right to Easter Island.

_____ 9. Statues that look like moai are found only in Peru and on Easter Island.

_____ 10. Ancient people might have sailed from Peru to Polynesia and then to Easter Island.

**Read the question, and write your answer.**

Why do some scientists believe Heyerdahl's idea that the first settlers to Easter Island came from Peru?

_____

_____

_____

**Chapter Quiz**

Name _____ Date _____

# *The Navel of the World*
## Chapter 6, "The Mystery of the Moai"

**Fill in the bubble beside the answer for each question.**

1. The islanders might have made moai to
   - Ⓐ scare away sailors.
   - Ⓑ make fun of their chiefs.
   - Ⓒ honor their ancestors.

2. The statues have
   - Ⓐ blue eyes.
   - Ⓑ short noses.
   - Ⓒ long ears.

3. Some moai may have been left unfinished because
   - Ⓐ the carvers got tired of carving.
   - Ⓑ the statues made the island too crowded.
   - Ⓒ the nobles wanted houses instead.

4. The people may have built Ahu Akivi to
   - Ⓐ greet sailors.
   - Ⓑ have meetings.
   - Ⓒ look at the stars.

**Read the question, and write your answer.**

Why do you think the seven moai at Ahu Akivi face the sunset during the equinox?

_____

_____

The Unexpected • Book 3

# Thinking and Writing

Name _____ Date _____

## *The Navel of the World*
### Think About It

**Write about or give an oral presentation for each question.**

1. Long ago some Polynesians left their homes to find a new place to live. If you were going to a new land, what would you take with you?

2. You have learned some theories about the moai. Why do you think the people of Easter Island made the huge statues?

3. Describe a tour of Easter Island.

## Write About It

**Choose one of the questions below. Write your answer on a sheet of paper.**

1. You've read several ideas about why ancient Easter Islanders built the moai. What kind of statue would you like to have near your home? Write a speech telling why the statue would be a good idea.

2. The books in this set are based on the theme **The Unexpected**. How does this book fit with the theme?

3. Complete the What I Know/What I Learned Chart for this book.

# Fluency Passages

## *The Navel of the World*

**Chapter 3** *page 9*

| | |
|---|---|
| *Next the carvers began chipping at the rock. They chipped until only | 12 |
| a little bit of rock was left between the moai and the wall. This held the | 28 |
| moai to the wall. It took a long time to carve the moai. Some were 40 feet | 45 |
| tall. Many were 15 tons or more. | 52 |
| When the statue was completed, the carvers broke the rock holding it | 64 |
| to the wall. Then they moved the moai to holes they had made. There they | 79 |
| decorated the moai. | 82 |
| The carvers added eyes made of stone. Some* moai were given *pukao*. | 94 |
| Pukao looks like a big stone hat, but it is really the statue's hair. | 108 |

**Chapter 6** *page 24*

| | |
|---|---|
| *Some people on the island wore big earrings. The earrings made | 11 |
| their ears long. Some people think the islanders with long ears were rich | 24 |
| nobles. The nobles may have made the people with short ears carve the | 37 |
| statues. The islanders with short ears may have become tired of carving | 49 |
| moai. That could be why some moai were not completed. | 59 |
| Other people think aliens from other planets landed on Easter Island. | 70 |
| They think the aliens were trapped on the island. Maybe the aliens helped | 83 |
| the islanders make the statues. But there* is not much reason to think this | 97 |
| is true. | 99 |

---

- The target rate for **The Unexpected** is 90 wcpm. The asterisks (*) mark 90 words.
- Listen to the student read the passage. Count the number of words read in one minute and the number of errors.
- For the reading rate, subtract the number of errors from the total number of words read.
- Have students enter their scores on their **Fluency Graph.** See page 9.

# Answer Key

## Building Background

Name _____ Date _____

*The Navel of the World*
**What You Know**
Write answers to these questions.

1. What are some famous landmarks in the United States? Where are they located? Why are they famous? Write your answers on a separate sheet of paper. **Accept reasonable responses.**

2. Begin the What I Know/What I Learned Chart for this book. Complete the What I Know portion.

3. Why do you think artists create statues? _____
   **Accept reasonable responses.**

4. If you had to move something that weighed 20 or 30 tons, how would you do it? **Accept reasonable responses.**

5. What everyday tools make our lives much easier today?
   **Accept reasonable responses.**

**Word Meanings**
*Definitions*
Look for these words as you read your chapter book. When you find one of these words, write its definition.

aliens: **beings that come from another world**
ancestors: **people who come earlier in a family; forefathers**
carve: **to shape by carefully cutting; sculpt**
equinox: **the two times of the year when day and night are the same length, 12 hours, all over Earth**
navel: **the central point**
statue: **form of a person or animal made from a solid material**

36 — The Unexpected • Book 3

### The Navel of the World

---

## Chapter Quiz

Name _____ Date _____

*The Navel of the World*
**Chapter 1, "The Navel of the World"**
Mark each statement *T* for true or *F* for false.

**T** 1. Easter Island has many stone statues.
**F** 2. Scientists know who built the statues.
**T** 3. Easter Island is small.
**F** 4. Easter Island is in the Atlantic Ocean.
**F** 5. The island is shaped like a circle.
**F** 6. The closest land to Easter Island is 4,000 miles away.
**T** 7. Easter Island was formed from three volcanoes.
**T** 8. The island's first settlers were probably Polynesians.
**F** 9. No plants grow on Easter Island.
**T** 10. The island people thought Easter Island was the middle of the world.

Read the question, and write your answer.

Describe the geography of Easter Island. _____
**Ideas: volcanoes, lush vegetation, fertile soil**

38 — The Unexpected • Book 3

### The Navel of the World

---

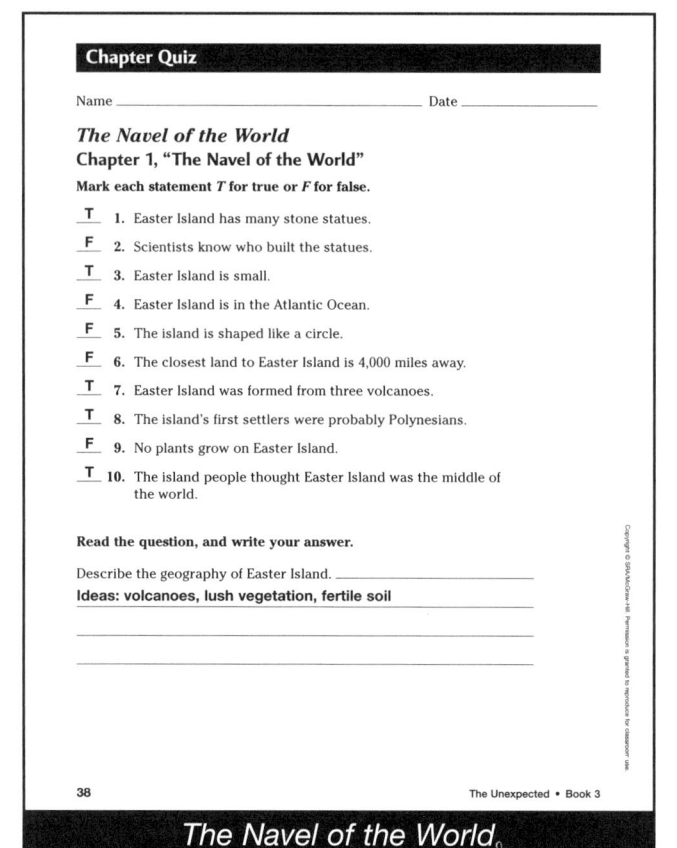

## Chapter Quiz

Name _____ Date _____

*The Navel of the World*
**Chapter 2, "Easter Island"**
Fill in the bubble beside the answer for each question.

1. Easter Island was named by
   Ⓐ a Polynesian king.
   ● a Dutch sea captain.
   Ⓒ an island chief.

2. In the 1800s, people from Peru
   Ⓐ built stone statues on the island.
   Ⓑ built towns on the island.
   ● took many of the islanders away.

3. Most of the statues, or *moai*,
   ● were destroyed.
   Ⓑ are still in good condition.
   Ⓒ were stolen.

4. The language and history of the island
   Ⓐ were kept in a safe place.
   ● have been lost for a long time.
   Ⓒ are known by people all over the world.

Read the question, and write your answer.

Why do we know so little about the history of Easter Island?
**Stone slabs that might provide information have been broken;**
**no one knows the language.**

The Unexpected • Book 3 — 39

### The Navel of the World

---

## Chapter Quiz

Name _____ Date _____

*The Navel of the World*
**Chapter 3, "Carving the Moai"**
Mark each statement *T* for true or *F* for false.

**T** 1. Soft rock from the volcanoes was good for carving.
**F** 2. The carvers worked at the top of a mountain.
**T** 3. The carvers started by drawing an outline on a rock wall.
**F** 4. Moai could be carved very quickly.
**T** 5. Carvers added stone eyes to the moai.
**F** 6. Pukao look like earrings.
**T** 7. Completed moai were moved to platforms.
**F** 8. The islanders used ahu to move the moai across the island.
**T** 9. There are still over 800 moai on Easter Island.
**T** 10. Many moai still stand in the crater where they were made.

Read the question, and write your answer.

What was the purpose of the moai? How big are they?
**No one knows why they were made; gigantic; some are 40 feet**
**tall and weigh 15 tons or more**

40 — The Unexpected • Book 3

### The Navel of the World

---

46                                    The Unexpected • Book 3

# Answer Key

## Chapter Quiz

Name _____ Date _____

*The Navel of the World*
Chapter 4, "Moving the Moai"

**Number the events in order from 1 to 5.**

_3_ Islanders told Thor Heyerdahl the moai had been dragged across the island.
_1_ Ancient islanders moved the moai across the island.
_5_ Heyerdahl and his helpers made a sled from two logs.
_2_ In 1955 Heyerdahl went to Easter Island.
_4_ Heyerdahl decided to try to move a moai.

**Number the events in order from 6 to 10.**

_10_ The people moved a ten-ton moai.
_8_ Using ropes, Heyerdahl and his helpers lowered the statue onto the sled.
_9_ Using ropes tied to the sled, people pulled the sled with the moai.
_6_ Heyerdahl and his helpers tied ropes to the sled.
_7_ People tied ropes to a statue.

**Read the question, and write your answer.**

Why might some people believe that the moai walked?
**A walking movement may have occurred when the moai were moved.**

The Unexpected • Book 3          41

## Chapter Quiz

Name _____ Date _____

*The Navel of the World*
Chapter 5, "Who Made the Moai?"

**Mark each statement *T* for true or *F* for false.**

_T_ 1. *Rapanui* is the term for the people and language of the island.
_F_ 2. The Rapanui are not related to the early islanders.
_T_ 3. The ancient islanders are still a mystery.
_F_ 4. Sweet potatoes show that the first islanders might have come from Polynesia.
_T_ 5. Heyerdahl tried to prove that Easter Islanders came from Peru.
_F_ 6. Heyerdahl sailed on a modern sailboat.
_F_ 7. Heyerdahl's boat drifted for many years.
_F_ 8. Heyerdahl drifted right to Easter Island.
_T_ 9. Statues that look like moai are found only in Peru and on Easter Island.
_T_ 10. Ancient people might have sailed from Peru to Polynesia and then to Easter Island.

**Read the question, and write your answer.**

Why do some scientists believe Heyerdahl's idea that the first settlers to Easter Island came from Peru?
**The only other statue in the world that looks like a moai is in Peru; sweet potatoes came from South America.**

42          The Unexpected • Book 3

## Chapter Quiz

Name _____ Date _____

*The Navel of the World*
Chapter 6, "The Mystery of the Moai"

**Fill in the bubble beside the answer for each question.**

1. The islanders might have made moai to
   Ⓐ scare away sailors.
   Ⓑ make fun of their chiefs.
   ● honor their ancestors.

2. The statues have
   Ⓐ blue eyes.
   Ⓑ short noses.
   ● long ears.

3. Some moai may have been left unfinished because
   ● the carvers got tired of carving.
   Ⓑ the statues made the island too crowded.
   Ⓒ the nobles wanted houses instead.

4. The people may have built Ahu Akivi to
   Ⓐ greet sailors.
   Ⓑ have meetings.
   ● look at the stars.

**Read the question, and write your answer.**

Why do you think the seven moai at Ahu Akivi face the sunset during the equinox?
**Answers will vary.**

The Unexpected • Book 3          43

## Thinking and Writing

Name _____ Date _____

*The Navel of the World*
**Think About It**

**Write about or give an oral presentation for each question.**

1. Long ago some Polynesians left their homes to find a new place to live. If you were going to a new land, what would you take with you?
   **Ideas: food, tools, books, skilled people**

2. You have learned some theories about the moai. Why do you think the people of Easter Island made the huge statues?
   **Ideas: to honor their ancestors; to please their kings**

3. Describe a tour of Easter Island. **Ideas: see the size of statues; fly or sail there; feel the isolation**

**Write About It**

**Choose one of the questions below. Write your answer on a sheet of paper.**

1. You've read several ideas about why ancient Easter Islanders built the moai. What kind of statue would you like to have near your home? Write a speech telling why the statue would be a good idea.

2. The books in this set are based on the theme **The Unexpected**. How does this book fit with the theme?

3. Complete the What I Know/What I Learned Chart for this book.

44          The Unexpected • Book 3

The Unexpected • Book 3          47

# Building Background

Name _____ Date _____

## *The Mountain Is on Fire!*
### What You Know

**Write answers to these questions.**

1. What types of natural disasters could occur in the region where you live? Why is your area vulnerable to these types of natural disasters?

   _____

   _____

2. Why do government officials issue warnings about potential natural disasters? _____

   _____

3. Why do volcanoes pose serious threats to those who live near them?

   _____

## Word Meanings
### *Matching*

**Look for these words as you read your chapter book. When you find a word, draw a line to connect the word with the correct definition.**

| | |
|---|---|
| eruption | melted rock from a volcano |
| lava | a hill or mountain with melted rock underneath |
| magma | an explosion that breaks through the surface of the earth |
| pressure | capable of action or movement; working |
| volcano | force of steadily pushing something else when the two are in direct contact |
| active | hot, liquid rock inside the earth |

48             The Unexpected • Book 4

# Word Lists

## *The Mountain Is on Fire!*

| | Unfamiliar Words | Word Meanings | Proper Nouns | |
|---|---|---|---|---|
| | commander<br>erupt<br>mountain<br>uncle | volcano | Mount Vesuvius<br>Pliny the Younger [PLI-nee]<br>Pompeii [pahm-PAY] | Chapter 1 |
| | building<br>buried<br>cough<br>huge<br>knew<br>large<br>ruin | | | Chapter 2 |
| | area<br>beautiful<br>earthquake<br>either<br>machine<br>place<br>scientist<br>sign<br>swept<br>warn<br>world | eruption<br>lava | April<br>March<br>Mount St. Helens<br>Native American<br>Washington | Chapter 3 |
| | angry<br>phone<br>rising<br>sure | | Dan Miller<br>David Johnston<br>Harry Truman | Chapter 4 |
| | break<br>gray<br>great<br>insect<br>liquid<br>material<br>pieces<br>soil | magma<br>pressure | | Chapter 5 |
| | gather<br>since | active | | Chapter 6 |

The Unexpected • Book 4     49

# Chapter Quiz

Name _____ Date _____

## *The Mountain Is on Fire!*
### Chapter 1, "The Volcano"

**Mark each statement *T* for true or *F* for false.**

____ 1. A dark cloud seemed to be stuck to the mountain.

____ 2. Pliny the Younger is telling this story.

____ 3. Pliny lived close to the mountain.

____ 4. His uncle told him not to go to the mountain.

____ 5. His uncle was also his teacher.

____ 6. His uncle went to save a woman in Pompeii.

____ 7. Pliny stayed home to do lessons.

____ 8. Pliny and his mother were not afraid for his uncle.

____ 9. This story took place just a few years ago.

____ 10. Pompeii was a town at the foot of Mount Vesuvius.

**Read the question, and write your answer.**

When and where does the story told in Chapter 1 take place?

_____

_____

# Chapter Quiz

Name _____ Date _____

## *The Mountain Is on Fire!*
### Chapter 2, "The Red Cloud"

**Number the events in order from 1 to 5.**

____ They saw a big cloud that was full of flames.

____ Buildings were shaking and falling all around them.

____ Pliny's mother started coughing because of the dust and ash.

____ A man came to help Pliny and his mother.

____ Pliny and his mother left the town.

**Number the events in order from 6 to 10.**

____ Pliny's mother told him to leave her behind.

____ The cloud lifted, and they could see the sun.

____ The air became black, and they could hear people crying.

____ He took her hand, and they sat down together.

____ Pompeii was a ruin. It was buried under ash.

**Read the question, and write your answer.**

What caused the death of Pliny the Elder? _____

_____

The Unexpected • Book 4

# Chapter Quiz

Name _____ Date _____

## *The Mountain Is on Fire!*
### Chapter 3, "Mount St. Helens Erupts"

**Fill in the bubble beside the answer for each question.**

1. Where is Mount St. Helens?
   - Ⓐ in Washington
   - Ⓑ in Italy, near Pompeii
   - Ⓒ in New York

2. What did scientists know was a bad sign?
   - Ⓐ Steam was rising from the mountain.
   - Ⓑ The mountain had deep blue lakes and streams.
   - Ⓒ both A and B

3. What did Native Americans call the mountain?
   - Ⓐ Mount St. Helens
   - Ⓑ the smoking mountain
   - Ⓒ hot top

4. What did the wind carry all over the world from Mount St. Helens?
   - Ⓐ fire
   - Ⓑ gases
   - Ⓒ ash

**Read the question, and write your answer.**

Contrast the appearance of Mount St. Helens before and after the volcano erupted. _____

_____

_____

# Chapter Quiz

Name _____ Date _____

## *The Mountain Is on Fire!*
### Chapter 4, "Some Stayed Behind"

**Mark each statement *T* for true or *F* for false.**

____ 1. Dan Miller was on his way to take pictures of Mount St. Helens.

____ 2. Miller was far from the mountain.

____ 3. Miller felt safe.

____ 4. Miller stayed on the mountain.

____ 5. Some people would not leave the mountain.

____ 6. David Johnston knew he could be killed.

____ 7. Johnston stayed because he did not want to leave his pets.

____ 8. Johnston said, "This is it!"

____ 9. Johnston stayed to make sure other people were safe.

____ 10. Harry Truman wanted to leave, but his truck ran out of gas.

**Read the question, and write your answer.**

Why might some people stay and others leave when they have been warned that a volcano might suddenly erupt?

_____

_____

_____

The Unexpected • Book 4

# Chapter Quiz

Name _____ Date _____

## *The Mountain Is on Fire!*
### Chapter 5, "Why Mountains Erupt"

**Fill in the bubble beside the answer for each question.**

1. What is a clue that a mountain may be a volcano?
   - Ⓐ size
   - Ⓑ cone shape
   - Ⓒ covered with snow

2. What happens to rock inside a volcano?
   - Ⓐ turns to stone
   - Ⓑ turns to liquid
   - Ⓒ turns to ice

3. What happens to the volcano if there is too much pressure?
   - Ⓐ It leaks hot gas.
   - Ⓑ It blows its top.
   - Ⓒ both A and B

4. What is magma called after it leaves a volcano?
   - Ⓐ cone
   - Ⓑ lava
   - Ⓒ gas

**Read the question, and write your answer.**

What happens to the land around a volcano after it erupts?

_____

_____

# Chapter Quiz

Name _____ Date _____

## *The Mountain Is on Fire!*
### Chapter 6, "Warnings Save Lives"

**Mark each statement *T* for true or *F* for false.**

____ 1. There are only ten active volcanoes in the world today.

____ 2. Volcanoes erupt every day.

____ 3. In A.D. 79, scientists knew Mount Vesuvius was going to erupt.

____ 4. When Mount Vesuvius erupted, 2,000 people died.

____ 5. When Mount St. Helens erupted, 2,000 people died.

____ 6. Warnings about Mount St. Helens did not save any lives.

____ 7. Small quakes are not a sign of danger.

____ 8. Big cracks show there is pressure inside a mountain.

____ 9. A volcano leaks gas before it erupts.

____ 10. Scientists no longer need to watch Mount St. Helens.

**Read the question, and write your answer.**

Why did so many people die when Mount Vesuvius erupted?

_____

_____

_____

The Unexpected • Book 4

# Thinking and Writing

Name _____ Date _____

## *The Mountain Is on Fire!*
## Think About It

**Write about or give an oral presentation for each question.**

1. Some people stayed when they were told Mount St. Helens was going to erupt. What would you have done? Why?

2. Johnston and Miller had dangerous jobs. Would you take a job that could cost you your life? Why or why not?

3. What are some ways scientists make the world a safer place?

## Write About It

**Choose one of the questions below. Write your answer on a sheet of paper.**

1. Imagine you are watching a volcano erupt. Tell what you see, what you hear, and what you feel.

2. Reread Chapter 5. In your own words, tell how a mountain blows its top. Tell what happens step by step. Use words such as first, then, and next to help show the different steps.

3. Complete the Compare and Contrast Diagram for this book.

# Fluency Passages

## *The Mountain Is on Fire!*

**Chapter 2** *pages 6 and 7*

| | |
|---|---:|
| *A man came to help us. He said we were in danger. He told us to | 16 |
| leave as quickly as we could. Buildings were falling all around us. Our | 29 |
| house was still all right, but not for long. | 38 |
| We knew we had to leave. We could see the huge cloud. It was full | 53 |
| of flames. | 55 |
| The burning cloud came closer to land. It was coming right at us! | 68 |
| Fine dust and ash fell from the sky. Mother started to cough. She told | 82 |
| me to leave her. | 86 |
| "I will die happy,"* she said, "if I know you did not die because of | 101 |
| me." | 102 |

**Chapter 5** *page 23*

| | |
|---|---:|
| *When magma comes out of a volcano, it is called "lava." Air makes | 13 |
| the lava thicker. Hot lava flows out of the volcano. It kills everything in its | 28 |
| path. | 29 |
| Over time, lava helps make the soil rich. After Mount St. Helens | 41 |
| erupted, the land looked as bare and gray as the moon. But within a year | 56 |
| things started to grow again. Little green plants shot up from the ash. | 69 |
| Today small trees grow everywhere. Flowers dot the land. Insects, | 79 |
| birds, and animals once again live on the mountain. | 88 |
| Will the* mountain stay silent? No one knows for sure. | 98 |

---

- The target rate for **The Unexpected** is 90 wcpm. The asterisks (*) mark 90 words.
- Listen to the student read the passage. Count the number of words read in one minute and the number of errors.
- For the reading rate, subtract the number of errors from the total number of words read.
- Have students enter their scores on their **Fluency Graph.** See page 9.

# Answer Key

## Building Background

Name _____ Date _____

*The Mountain Is on Fire!*
**What You Know**
Write answers to these questions.

1. What types of natural disasters could occur in the region where you live? Why is your area vulnerable to these types of natural disasters?
   **Answers will vary depending upon location.**

2. Why do government officials issue warnings about potential natural disasters? **to give people time to prepare, secure their property, leave the area**

3. Why do volcanoes pose serious threats to those who live near them?
   **highly destructive**

**Word Meanings**
*Matching*
Look for these words as you read your chapter book. When you find a word, draw a line to connect the word with the correct definition.

- eruption — melted rock from a volcano
- lava — a hill or mountain with melted rock underneath
- magma — an explosion that breaks through the surface of the earth
- pressure — capable of action or movement; working
- volcano — force of steadily pushing something else when the two are in direct contact
- active — hot, liquid rock inside the earth

48    The Unexpected • Book 4

### The Mountain Is on Fire!

---

## Chapter Quiz

Name _____ Date _____

*The Mountain Is on Fire!*
**Chapter 1, "The Volcano"**
Mark each statement *T* for true or *F* for false.

- **T** 1. A dark cloud seemed to be stuck to the mountain.
- **T** 2. Pliny the Younger is telling this story.
- **F** 3. Pliny lived close to the mountain.
- **F** 4. His uncle told him not to go to the mountain.
- **T** 5. His uncle was also his teacher.
- **T** 6. His uncle went to save a woman in Pompeii.
- **T** 7. Pliny stayed home to do lessons.
- **F** 8. Pliny and his mother were not afraid for his uncle.
- **F** 9. This story took place just a few years ago.
- **T** 10. Pompeii was a town at the foot of Mount Vesuvius.

Read the question, and write your answer.

When and where does the story told in Chapter 1 take place?
**A.D. 79; Pompeii, Italy**

50    The Unexpected • Book 4

### The Mountain Is on Fire!

---

## Chapter Quiz

Name _____ Date _____

*The Mountain Is on Fire!*
**Chapter 2, "The Red Cloud"**
Number the events in order from 1 to 5.

- **4** They saw a big cloud that was full of flames.
- **2** Buildings were shaking and falling all around them.
- **5** Pliny's mother started coughing because of the dust and ash.
- **1** A man came to help Pliny and his mother.
- **3** Pliny and his mother left the town.

Number the events in order from 6 to 10.

- **6** Pliny's mother told him to leave her behind.
- **9** The cloud lifted, and they could see the sun.
- **8** The air became black, and they could hear people crying.
- **7** He took her hand, and they sat down together.
- **10** Pompeii was a ruin. It was buried under ash.

Read the question, and write your answer.

What caused the death of Pliny the Elder? **the thick dust and gas stopped his breathing**

The Unexpected • Book 4    51

### The Mountain Is on Fire!

---

## Chapter Quiz

Name _____ Date _____

*The Mountain Is on Fire!*
**Chapter 3, "Mount St. Helens Erupts"**
Fill in the bubble beside the answer for each question.

1. Where is Mount St. Helens?
   - ● in Washington
   - Ⓑ in Italy, near Pompeii
   - Ⓒ in New York

2. What did scientists know was a bad sign?
   - ● Steam was rising from the mountain.
   - Ⓑ The mountain had deep blue lakes and streams.
   - Ⓒ both A and B

3. What did Native Americans call the mountain?
   - Ⓐ Mount St. Helens
   - ● the smoking mountain
   - Ⓒ hot top

4. What did the wind carry all over the world from Mount St. Helens?
   - Ⓐ fire
   - Ⓑ gases
   - ● ash

Read the question, and write your answer.

Contrast the appearance of Mount St. Helens before and after the volcano erupted. **before: flowers, birds, clear blue streams and lakes; after: sky turned black; people, animals, and vegetation killed; rivers filled with lava; roads, bridges swept away**

52    The Unexpected • Book 4

### The Mountain Is on Fire!

---

58      The Unexpected • Book 4

# Answer Key

## Chapter Quiz

Name _____ Date _____

*The Mountain Is on Fire!*
**Chapter 4, "Some Stayed Behind"**
Mark each statement *T* for true or *F* for false.

__T__ 1. Dan Miller was on his way to take pictures of Mount St. Helens.
__T__ 2. Miller was far from the mountain.
__F__ 3. Miller felt safe.
__F__ 4. Miller stayed on the mountain.
__T__ 5. Some people would not leave the mountain.
__T__ 6. David Johnston knew he could be killed.
__F__ 7. Johnston stayed because he did not want to leave his pets.
__T__ 8. Johnston said, "This is it!"
__T__ 9. Johnston stayed to make sure other people were safe.
__F__ 10. Harry Truman wanted to leave, but his truck ran out of gas.

Read the question, and write your answer.

Why might some people stay and others leave when they have been warned that a volcano might suddenly erupt?
**Ideas: leave to protect selves and belongings; stay to help others; they don't believe warnings; cannot leave for a variety of reasons**

The Unexpected • Book 4 — 53

### The Mountain Is on Fire!

## Chapter Quiz

Name _____ Date _____

*The Mountain Is on Fire!*
**Chapter 5, "Why Mountains Erupt"**
Fill in the bubble beside the answer for each question.

1. What is a clue that a mountain may be a volcano?
   Ⓐ size
   ● cone shape
   Ⓒ covered with snow

2. What happens to rock inside a volcano?
   Ⓐ turns to stone
   ● turns to liquid
   Ⓒ turns to ice

3. What happens to the volcano if there is too much pressure?
   Ⓐ It leaks hot gas.
   Ⓑ It blows its top.
   ● both A and B

4. What is magma called after it leaves a volcano?
   Ⓐ cone
   ● lava
   Ⓒ gas

Read the question, and write your answer.

What happens to the land around a volcano after it erupts?
**everything is killed and covered in ash**

54 — The Unexpected • Book 4

### The Mountain Is on Fire!

## Chapter Quiz

Name _____ Date _____

*The Mountain Is on Fire!*
**Chapter 6, "Warnings Save Lives"**
Mark each statement *T* for true or *F* for false.

__F__ 1. There are only ten active volcanoes in the world today.
__T__ 2. Volcanoes erupt every day.
__F__ 3. In A.D. 79, scientists knew Mount Vesuvius was going to erupt.
__T__ 4. When Mount Vesuvius erupted, 2,000 people died.
__F__ 5. When Mount St. Helens erupted, 2,000 people died.
__F__ 6. Warnings about Mount St. Helens did not save any lives.
__F__ 7. Small quakes are not a sign of danger.
__T__ 8. Big cracks show there is pressure inside a mountain.
__T__ 9. A volcano leaks gas before it erupts.
__F__ 10. Scientists no longer need to watch Mount St. Helens.

Read the question, and write your answer.

Why did so many people die when Mount Vesuvius erupted?
**had no advance warning and no way to escape**

The Unexpected • Book 4 — 55

### The Mountain Is on Fire!

## Thinking and Writing

Name _____ Date _____

*The Mountain Is on Fire!*
**Think About It**
Write about or give an oral presentation for each question.

1. Some people stayed when they were told Mount St. Helens was going to erupt. What would you have done? Why?
   **Accept reasonable responses.**

2. Johnston and Miller had dangerous jobs. Would you take a job that could cost you your life? Why or why not?
   **Idea: Some jobs are dangerous but necessary, such as police officers and firefighters.**

3. What are some ways scientists make the world a safer place?
   **They develop equipment that warns about storms or earthquakes.**

**Write About It**
Choose one of the questions below. Write your answer on a sheet of paper.

1. Imagine you are watching a volcano erupt. Tell what you see, what you hear, and what you feel.
2. Reread Chapter 5. In your own words, tell how a mountain blows its top. Tell what happens step by step. Use words such as first, then, and next to help show the different steps.
3. Complete the Compare and Contrast Diagram for this book.

56 — The Unexpected • Book 4

### The Mountain Is on Fire!

The Unexpected • Book 4 — 59

# Building Background

Name _____ Date _____

## *Atlantis: Land of Mystery*
## What You Know

**Write answers to these questions.**

1. Describe a perfect place to live. What would it be like? How would people spend their time? Write your answer on a separate piece of paper.

2. What kinds of scientists study the past and ancient peoples? _____

3. Do you think it is possible for an entire island to be hidden under the sea? Explain your answer. _____

4. What kinds of machines are needed for exploration of areas deep under the sea? _____

## Word Meanings
### *Synonyms and Antonyms*

**Look for these words as you read your chapter book. When you find one of these words, write its definition, and then write a synonym for it.**

artifacts: _____

erupted: _____

pyramid: _____

**When you find one of these words, write its definition, and then write an antonym for it.**

island: _____

survivors: _____

volcano: _____

# Word Lists

## Atlantis: Land of Mystery

| | Unfamiliar Words | Word Meanings | Proper Nouns | |
|---|---|---|---|---|
| **Chapter 1** | building, canal, climate, coconut, field, gods, learn, music, mystery, perfect, whenever, wonderful, world | island | Ana, Atlantic Ocean, Atlantis, Grandpa Carlos, Mexico | |
| **Chapter 2** | apart, destroyed, knew, lava, night, safety, second | erupted, volcano | Mayan | |
| **Chapter 3** | ancient, great, listened, movie, true, wrote | | Egypt, Greece, Ignatius Donnelly, Plato, Solon [SOH-lan] | |
| **Chapter 4** | dangerous, different, machine, secret, sure, survived, taught | pyramid, survivors | Aztlan [Ahst-LAHN], Egyptians, Mexicans, Pacific Ocean | |
| **Chapter 5** | changed, existed, known | artifacts | Antarctica, Bahamas, Minoan, Thera [THEE-rah] | |
| **Chapter 6** | human, remain, scientist, search, someday | | *Titanic* | |

The Unexpected • Book 5

# Chapter Quiz

Name _____ Date _____

## *Atlantis: Land of Mystery*
### Chapter 1, "Life in Atlantis"

**Fill in the bubble beside the answer for each question.**

1. Where do Ana and Carlos live?
   - Ⓐ Mexico
   - Ⓑ Atlantis
   - Ⓒ United States

2. Which word best describes life in Atlantis?
   - Ⓐ hard
   - Ⓑ hot
   - Ⓒ perfect

3. Atlantis was
   - Ⓐ an ocean.
   - Ⓑ an island.
   - Ⓒ a garden.

4. How long ago do people think Atlantis existed?
   - Ⓐ 100 years
   - Ⓑ 1,000 years
   - Ⓒ 10,000 years

**Read the question, and write your answer.**

What kinds of jobs did people do on Atlantis? _____

_____

_____

**Chapter Quiz**

Name _____ Date _____

## *Atlantis: Land of Mystery*
### Chapter 2, "The End of Atlantis"

**Number the events in order from 1 to 5.**

____ Ana thought about Atlantis while she ate.

____ Thunder crashed.

____ Ana washed the dinner dishes.

____ The little boys went to bed.

____ Ana's brothers started to cry.

**Number the events in order from 6 to 10.**

____ Atlantis sank into the sea.

____ A big wave covered the island.

____ For years, life in Atlantis was perfect.

____ A volcano erupted.

____ Some of the people fell into the open ground.

**Read the question, and write your answer.**

What brought about the end of Atlantis, and how did some people manage to survive?

_____

_____

_____

The Unexpected • Book 5

# Chapter Quiz

Name _____ Date _____

## *Atlantis: Land of Mystery*
### Chapter 3, "An Ancient Legend"

**Fill in the bubble beside the answer for each question.**

1. Who told Ana the story of Atlantis?
   - Ⓐ Carlos
   - Ⓑ Plato
   - Ⓒ Solon

2. Who was the first person to write about Atlantis?
   - Ⓐ Ana
   - Ⓑ Donnelly
   - Ⓒ Plato

3. Where did Plato live?
   - Ⓐ Mexico
   - Ⓑ Greece
   - Ⓒ Atlantis

4. Why might Plato have made up the story?
   - Ⓐ just for fun
   - Ⓑ to teach a lesson
   - Ⓒ to tell a lie

**Read the question, and write your answer.**

Why did people become interested in Atlantis in the late 1800s?

_____

_____

The Unexpected • Book 5

# Chapter Quiz

Name _____ Date _____

## *Atlantis: Land of Mystery*
## Chapter 4, "Survivors"

**Fill in the bubble beside the answer for each question.**

1. How could someone have survived the end of Atlantis?
   - Ⓐ by running away
   - Ⓑ by sailing away
   - Ⓒ by riding away on an elephant

2. What might the Egyptians have learned from Atlantis?
   - Ⓐ how to move water
   - Ⓑ how to lift heavy stones
   - Ⓒ both A and B

3. Where are pyramids found today?
   - Ⓐ Mexico
   - Ⓑ Egypt
   - Ⓒ both A and B

4. Where might the first Maya have come from?
   - Ⓐ the sky
   - Ⓑ Egypt
   - Ⓒ Atlantis

**Read the question, and write your answer.**

Why do some people believe that sailors from Atlantis traveled to both Egypt and Mexico?

_____
_____
_____

The Unexpected • Book 5

# Chapter Quiz

Name _____  Date _____

## *Atlantis: Land of Mystery*
## Chapter 5, "Could Atlantis Be Real?"

**Mark each statement *T* for true or *F* for false.**

____ 1. We do not know if Atlantis really existed.

____ 2. We do not know if Thera really existed.

____ 3. Minoan people lived on Thera.

____ 4. Thera was an island where a volcano erupted.

____ 5. The Minoans knew how to do great things.

____ 6. The Egyptians traded with the Minoans.

____ 7. We know the story of Thera became the story of Atlantis.

____ 8. We know Atlantis was near Antarctica.

____ 9. We must find the lost island to prove where it was.

____ 10. We can learn about the past from artifacts.

**Read the question, and write your answer.**

Why do some people believe that Thera was Atlantis?

_____

_____

_____

**Chapter Quiz**

Name _____ Date _____

## *Atlantis: Land of Mystery*
### Chapter 6, "The Search Goes On"

**Mark each statement *T* for true or *F* for false.**

_____ 1. Many people have tried to find Atlantis.

_____ 2. So far no one has found Atlantis.

_____ 3. In 1968 something strange was found under water near the Bahamas.

_____ 4. Scientists said the wall had been made by humans.

_____ 5. The wall was too new to be from Atlantis.

_____ 6. New machines may help us find Atlantis.

_____ 7. New machines may prove Atlantis never existed.

_____ 8. Earth's crust never moves.

_____ 9. People are now able to search the whole ocean floor.

_____ 10. To some people, Atlantis means happiness and great riches.

**Read the question, and write your answer.**

Why do some people believe that Atlantis might rise again from the ocean?

_____

_____

The Unexpected • Book 5

# Thinking and Writing

Name _____ Date _____

## *Atlantis: Land of Mystery*
### Think About It

**Write about or give an oral presentation for each question.**

1. Do you think we should keep spending time and money looking for Atlantis? Why or why not? _____

2. What could we learn if we found Atlantis? _____

3. Is this story fiction or nonfiction? Explain your answer.

## Write About It

**Choose one of the questions below. Write your answer on a sheet of paper.**

1. Pretend you are a sailor from Atlantis. You have been away, and now you are sailing home. You see bad things happening on the island. Tell what you see and how you feel.

2. Write two paragraphs about life in Atlantis. In the first paragraph tell about the things that were good. In the next paragraph tell about the hard things.

3. Pretend you are Ana. Write a letter to a friend telling about Atlantis. Describe what Atlantis is like. Tell why you would like to visit Atlantis.

4. Complete the Genres Chart for this book.

# Fluency Passages

## *Atlantis: Land of Mystery*

**Chapter 1** *page 2*

| | |
|---|---:|
| *"No one knows where it is now," Carlos said. "Some think it was in | 14 |
| the middle of the Atlantic Ocean more than 10,000 years ago." | 25 |
| "No way!" Ana yelled. "There is no land there." | 34 |
| "Not now," Carlos said, "but Atlantis used to be there. It had | 46 |
| everything. The climate was perfect. There was rain when it was needed. | 58 |
| The people made canals that carried water to the fields. The canals made | 71 |
| farming easy. So there was a lot of food. Some food was free." | 84 |
| Working had made Ana hungry. | 89 |
| "What* kinds of food did they have?" Ana asked. | 98 |

**Chapter 2** *page 7*

| | |
|---|---:|
| *"I'm not scared," Ana thought. But she sat close to Grandpa Carlos. | 12 |
| Ana's mom and dad put the boys to bed. Then Grandpa Carlos began | 25 |
| telling more about Atlantis. | 29 |
| "Maybe the last night in Atlantis began like this," he began. Ana was | 42 |
| still. She wanted to know what happened to Atlantis. | 51 |
| "For years Atlantis was nearly perfect," Carlos said. "Then the people | 62 |
| became greedy. They wanted more and more. They took what they wanted. | 74 |
| They were mean. The gods stopped smiling. | 81 |
| "No one knew Atlantis was about to be destroyed.* Then bad things | 93 |
| started to happen all at once." | 99 |

---

- The target rate for **The Unexpected** is 90 wcpm. The asterisks (*) mark 90 words.
- Listen to the student read the passage. Count the number of words read in one minute and the number of errors.
- For the reading rate, subtract the number of errors from the total number of words read.
- Have students enter their scores on their **Fluency Graph.** See page 9.

# Answer Key

## Building Background

Name _____ Date _____

**Atlantis: Land of Mystery**
**What You Know**
Write answers to these questions.

1. Describe a perfect place to live. What would it be like? How would people spend their time? Write your answer on a separate piece of paper.
2. What kinds of scientists study the past and ancient peoples?
   **archaeologists, anthropologists**
3. Do you think it is possible for an entire island to be hidden under the sea? Explain your answer.
   **Accept reasonable responses.**
4. What kinds of machines are needed for exploration of areas deep under the sea? **submarines, unmanned deep sea explorers**

**Word Meanings**
*Synonyms and Antonyms*
Look for these words as you read your chapter book. When you find one of these words, write its definition, and then write a synonym for it.
artifacts: **simple objects made by humans that represent their culture; synonyms: tools, ornaments**
erupted: **burst forth, broke through the surface; synonym: exploded**
pyramid: **a massive structure with a square base and four triangular sides that meet in a point; synonym: triangular cone**

When you find one of these words, write its definition, and then write an antonym for it.
island: **area of land surrounded by water; antonym: continent, mainland**
survivors: **those who remain alive; antonym: victims, fatalities**
volcano: **a hill or mountain with an opening from which melted or hot rock and steam come out; antonym: a plain or a peaceful area**

*Atlantis: Land of Mystery*

---

## Chapter Quiz

Name _____ Date _____

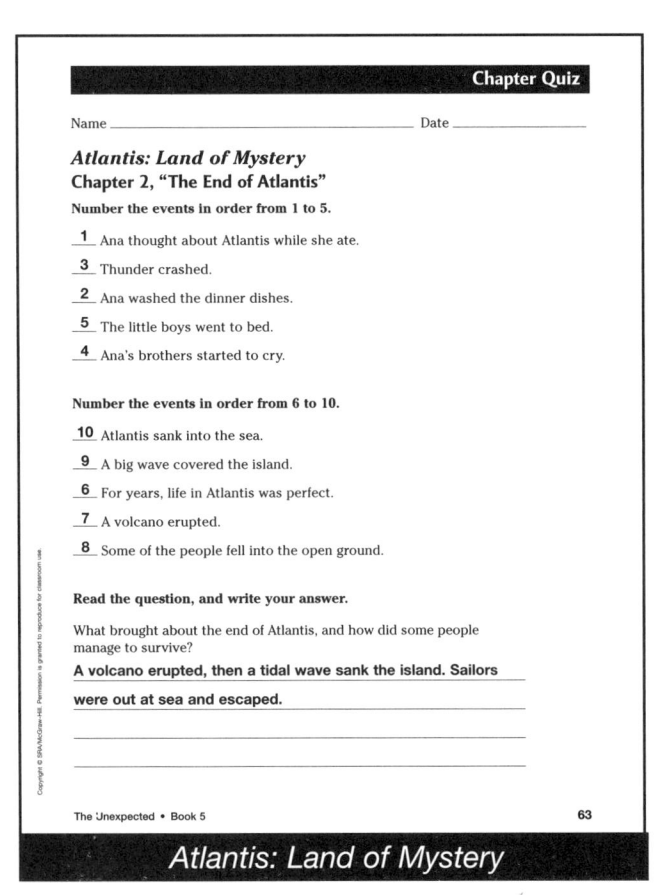

**Atlantis: Land of Mystery**
Chapter 1, "Life in Atlantis"
Fill in the bubble beside the answer for each question.

1. Where do Ana and Carlos live?
   ● Mexico
   Ⓑ Atlantis
   Ⓒ United States
2. Which word best describes life in Atlantis?
   Ⓐ hard
   Ⓑ hot
   ● perfect
3. Atlantis was
   Ⓐ an ocean.
   ● an island.
   Ⓒ a garden.
4. How long ago do people think Atlantis existed?
   Ⓐ 100 years
   Ⓑ 1,000 years
   ● 10,000 years

Read the question, and write your answer.
What kinds of jobs did people do on Atlantis? **Ideas: farmed, herded animals, built magnificent buildings, worked with gold and silver, sailed, traded; some were soldiers, teachers**

*Atlantis: Land of Mystery*

---

## Chapter Quiz

Name _____ Date _____

**Atlantis: Land of Mystery**
Chapter 2, "The End of Atlantis"
Number the events in order from 1 to 5.
- **1** Ana thought about Atlantis while she ate.
- **3** Thunder crashed.
- **2** Ana washed the dinner dishes.
- **5** The little boys went to bed.
- **4** Ana's brothers started to cry.

Number the events in order from 6 to 10.
- **10** Atlantis sank into the sea.
- **9** A big wave covered the island.
- **6** For years, life in Atlantis was perfect.
- **7** A volcano erupted.
- **8** Some of the people fell into the open ground.

Read the question, and write your answer.
What brought about the end of Atlantis, and how did some people manage to survive?
**A volcano erupted, then a tidal wave sank the island. Sailors were out at sea and escaped.**

*Atlantis: Land of Mystery*

---

## Chapter Quiz

Name _____ Date _____

**Atlantis: Land of Mystery**
Chapter 3, "An Ancient Legend"
Fill in the bubble beside the answer for each question.

1. Who told Ana the story of Atlantis?
   ● Carlos
   Ⓑ Plato
   Ⓒ Solon
2. Who was the first person to write about Atlantis?
   Ⓐ Ana
   Ⓑ Donnelly
   ● Plato
3. Where did Plato live?
   Ⓐ Mexico
   ● Greece
   Ⓒ Atlantis
4. Why might Plato have made up the story?
   Ⓐ just for fun
   ● to teach a lesson
   Ⓒ to tell a lie

Read the question, and write your answer.
Why did people become interested in Atlantis in the late 1800s?
**Ignatius Donnelly wrote a book about Atlantis that rekindled interest in the lost island.**

*Atlantis: Land of Mystery*

# Answer Key

---

**Chapter Quiz**

Name _____ Date _____

*Atlantis: Land of Mystery*
Chapter 4, "Survivors"

Fill in the bubble beside the answer for each question.

1. How could someone have survived the end of Atlantis?
   - Ⓐ by running away
   - ● by sailing away
   - Ⓒ by riding away on an elephant

2. What might the Egyptians have learned from Atlantis?
   - Ⓐ how to move water
   - Ⓑ how to lift heavy stones
   - ● both A and B

3. Where are pyramids found today?
   - Ⓐ Mexico
   - Ⓑ Egypt
   - ● both A and B

4. Where might the first Maya have come from?
   - Ⓐ the sky
   - Ⓑ Egypt
   - ● Atlantis

Read the question, and write your answer.

Why do some people believe that sailors from Atlantis traveled to both Egypt and Mexico?

Ideas: Like people of Atlantis, Egyptians built water canals and worked with gold; both Egyptians and Mexicans built pyramids; *Aztlan* is similar to the word *Atlantis*.

*Atlantis: Land of Mystery*

---

**Chapter Quiz**

Name _____ Date _____

*Atlantis: Land of Mystery*
Chapter 5, "Could Atlantis Be Real?"

Mark each statement *T* for true or *F* for false.

- T  1. We do not know if Atlantis really existed.
- F  2. We do not know if Thera really existed.
- T  3. Minoan people lived on Thera.
- T  4. Thera was an island where a volcano erupted.
- T  5. The Minoans knew how to do great things.
- T  6. The Egyptians traded with the Minoans.
- F  7. We know the story of Thera became the story of Atlantis.
- F  8. We know Atlantis was near Antarctica.
- T  9. We must find the lost island to prove where it was.
- T  10. We can learn about the past from artifacts.

Read the question, and write your answer.

Why do some people believe that Thera was Atlantis?

Ideas: many similarities; volcano destroyed Thera; Minoans living on Thera had an advanced culture, did many things well; traded with the Egyptians

*Atlantis: Land of Mystery*

---

**Chapter Quiz**

Name _____ Date _____

*Atlantis: Land of Mystery*
Chapter 6, "The Search Goes On"

Mark each statement *T* for true or *F* for false.

- T  1. Many people have tried to find Atlantis.
- T  2. So far no one has found Atlantis.
- T  3. In 1968 something strange was found under water near the Bahamas.
- F  4. Scientists said the wall had been made by humans.
- T  5. The wall was too new to be from Atlantis.
- T  6. New machines may help us find Atlantis.
- T  7. New machines may prove Atlantis never existed.
- F  8. Earth's crust never moves.
- F  9. People are now able to search the whole ocean floor.
- T  10. To some people, Atlantis means happiness and great riches.

Read the question, and write your answer.

Why do some people believe that Atlantis might rise again from the ocean?

As Earth's crust moves, land can be pushed up from the ocean floor.

*Atlantis: Land of Mystery*

---

**Thinking and Writing**

Name _____ Date _____

*Atlantis: Land of Mystery*
Think About It

Write about or give an oral presentation for each question.

1. Do you think we should keep spending time and money looking for Atlantis? Why or why not? Ideas: No, we should spend money on practical things; yes, we could learn a lot from Atlantis.

2. What could we learn if we found Atlantis? Answers will vary.

3. Is this story fiction or nonfiction? Explain your answer.
   Ideas: Carlos and Ana are fictional. Plato was a real person. No one knows if Atlantis existed, but it is true that people wrote about it.

**Write About It**

Choose one of the questions below. Write your answer on a sheet of paper.

1. Pretend you are a sailor from Atlantis. You have been away, and now you are sailing home. You see bad things happening on the island. Tell what you see and how you feel.

2. Write two paragraphs about life in Atlantis. In the first paragraph tell about the things that were good. In the next paragraph tell about the hard things.

3. Pretend you are Ana. Write a letter to a friend telling about Atlantis. Describe what Atlantis is like. Tell why you would like to visit Atlantis.

4. Complete the Genres Chart for this book.

*Atlantis: Land of Mystery*

---

The Unexpected • Book 5

# Building Background

Name _____ Date _____

## *Master of Disaster*
## What You Know

**Write answers to these questions.**

1. Use a dictionary to write the meaning of these words: *extreme, disaster, natural, man-made.* _____
_____
_____

2. List eight different kinds of disasters, both natural and man-made. Circle the natural disasters. Put a box around the man-made ones.
_____
_____

3. What kinds of natural disasters have occurred in the region where you live? What safety rules did you follow during those disasters?
_____
_____

## Word Meanings
### Synonyms
**Look for these words as you read your chapter book. When you find one of these words, write a synonym for it.**

during: _____

huge: _____

nice: _____

push: _____

whole: _____

worse: _____

# Word Lists

## *Master of Disaster*

| Unfamiliar Words | Word Meanings | Proper Nouns | |
|---|---|---|---|
| basement<br>cause<br>extremes<br>nature<br>often<br>quarter<br>waterspouts | nice<br>push | France<br>Rhode Island | Chapter 1 |
| buildings<br>cities<br>city<br>places | worse | Europe | Chapter 2 |
| face<br>metal<br>weather | whole | | Chapter 3 |
| flood<br>force<br>learn<br>levees<br>shoreline<br>surges | huge | Gulf of Mexico<br>Hurricane Katrina<br>New Orleans<br>United States | Chapter 4 |
| earthquakes<br>ripples<br>tidal<br>tsunamis | during | Alaska<br>Indian Ocean | Chapter 5 |
| continents<br>fault<br>machines<br>mantle<br>movements<br>stronger | | California<br>Earth<br>San Francisco | Chapter 6 |

The Unexpected • Book 6

# Chapter Quiz

Name _____ Date _____

## *Master of Disaster*
### Chapter 1, "Tornadoes"

**Mark each statement *T* for true or *F* for false.**

____ 1. Tornadoes are often called "twisters."

____ 2. Tornadoes are formed when hot air from the ground mixes with hot air in the sky.

____ 3. Cold air from the ground pushes spinning air up.

____ 4. Winds in a tornado can reach up to 900 miles an hour.

____ 5. It is unusual for a tornado to pick up things as large as cars and houses.

____ 6. One tornado sucked 30 cows into the sky, but the cows were not killed.

____ 7. Tornadoes usually do not smash things to bits.

____ 8. If you are home during a tornado, it is best to run to the basement.

____ 9. If you are driving when a tornado hits, it is best to try to outrun the tornado.

____ 10. *Waterspouts* are tornadoes that form over lakes or seas.

**Read the question, and write your answer.**

Why did it once rain fish in Rhode Island and toads in France?

_____

_____

**Chapter Quiz**

Name _____ Date _____

## *Master of Disaster*
## Chapter 2, "The Big Heat"

**Fill in the bubble beside the answer for each question.**

1. Heat in a city is worse than heat in a small town because
   - Ⓐ tall buildings keep cool winds out.
   - Ⓑ bricks and streets hold in the heat from sunlight.
   - Ⓒ both A and B

2. Air "bumps" usually form over
   - Ⓐ open fields.
   - Ⓑ small towns.
   - Ⓒ big cities.

3. You can stay cool at home by
   - Ⓐ keeping the shades up during the day.
   - Ⓑ drinking lots of water.
   - Ⓒ not using the fan.

4. Which group of people is most at risk of getting sick from the heat?
   - Ⓐ middle-aged people
   - Ⓑ teenagers
   - Ⓒ older people

**Read the question, and write your answer.**

What are three things you can do to stay cool in very hot weather?

_____

_____

_____

The Unexpected • Book 6

# Chapter Quiz

Name _____ Date _____

## *Master of Disaster*
## Chapter 3, "C-C-Cold"

**Fill in the bubble beside the answer for each question.**

1. Very cold weather can be
   - Ⓐ just as bad as very hot weather.
   - Ⓑ as cold as 10°F.
   - Ⓒ not as bad with the wind blowing.

2. In very cold weather
   - Ⓐ your face, hands, or feet can freeze.
   - Ⓑ your skin can start to look like wax.
   - Ⓒ both A and B

3. When your whole body gets too cold you
   - Ⓐ shiver a lot.
   - Ⓑ have lots of energy.
   - Ⓒ both A and B

4. Cold-weather outfits
   - Ⓐ should not be too heavy.
   - Ⓑ should keep you dry and away from the wind.
   - Ⓒ work better when they are wet.

**Read the question, and write your answer.**

Why is licking a metal pole in freezing weather a bad idea?

_____

_____

# Chapter Quiz

Name _____ Date _____

## *Master of Disaster*
## Chapter 4, "Storm Surges"

**Number the events in order from 1 to 5.**

____ The water sank into the ground, leaving salt behind.

____ Seawater smashed buildings and flooded farms.

____ During Hurricane Katrina, huge waves went over the levees.

____ No plants will grow there for years and years.

____ Seawater killed most of the plants.

**Mark each statement *T* for true or *F* for false.**

____ 1. The disaster in New Orleans was the result of a hurricane combined with a flood.

____ 2. Seawater helps plants grow because of the salt.

____ 3. Hurricane Katrina was one of the worst disasters to happen in the United States.

____ 4. Removing the wetlands and building a harbor for ships was a good idea.

**Read the question, and write your answer.**

What had been done in New Orleans that made the damage from Hurricane Katrina worse than other storms?

_____

_____

_____

The Unexpected • Book 6

# Chapter Quiz

Name _____ Date _____

## *Master of Disaster*
### Chapter 5, "Tsunamis"

**Number the events in order from 1 to 5.**

____ Shock waves moved through deep water and formed waves on top of the water.

____ Near the shore, the waves became huge walls of water.

____ In minutes, more than 250,000 people died.

____ The waves roared in and smashed everything in their path.

____ In 2004 there was an earthquake deep in the Indian Ocean.

**Mark each statement *T* for true or *F* for false.**

____ 1. Tidal waves are not the same as tsunamis.

____ 2. Tsunamis can be caused by earthquakes.

____ 3. A tsunami in Alaska was caused by a huge chunk of rock that fell into the water.

____ 4. The tsunami in Alaska killed many people.

**Read the question, and write your answer.**

What should you do if you are by the sea and the water suddenly leaves the shore and doesn't come back?

_____

_____

_____

**Chapter Quiz**

Name _____ Date _____

## *Master of Disaster*
### Chapter 6, "Earthquakes"

**Mark each statement *T* for true or *F* for false.**

___ 1. Earth is not hard all the way through.

___ 2. The mass of red-hot, melted rock is called the "crust."

___ 3. The continents lie on huge blocks of crust called "plates."

___ 4. The continents are moving several feet every year.

___ 5. If you are in an earthquake, you should stand beside a window.

___ 6. The biggest fault line in the United States is in California.

___ 7. The worst earthquake ever to hit the United States was in Northridge in 1994.

___ 8. Fighting fires after an earthquake can be very difficult because water mains can break during the earthquake.

___ 9. There are machines that can sense very tiny movements in Earth's crust.

___ 10. People are more likely than animals to know an earthquake is coming.

**Read the question, and write your answer.**

What causes an earthquake? Use the terms *mantle, crust,* and *plates* in your answer.

_____

_____

_____

The Unexpected • Book 6

# Thinking and Writing

Name _____ Date _____

## *Master of Disaster*
### Think About It

**Write about or give an oral presentation for each question.**

1. Compare tornadoes with hurricanes. How are they alike? How are they different? _____

2. How are natural and man-made disasters alike? How are they different? Which do you think are worse and why? _____

3. Make a list of extremes of nature this book tells about. For each extreme, describe how it affects people and list any warnings people may have. Which extreme would be easiest to avoid? _____

4. How could the damage to New Orleans from Hurricane Katrina, the heat extremes in cities, and the San Francisco earthquake be both man-made and natural disasters? _____

### Write About It

**Choose one of the questions below. Write your answer on a sheet of paper.**

1. Write a *Master of Disaster Safety Booklet* describing how to be safe in a tornado, a hurricane, extreme heat and cold, a tsunami, and an earthquake.

2. Pretend you lived through one of the natural disasters in this book. Write a letter telling what happened to you. Tell about any warning you had and how you protected yourself.

3. Complete the Content Web for this book.

# Fluency Passages

## *Master of Disaster*

**Chapter 1** *page 4*

| | |
|---|---:|
| *Most tornadoes just smash things to bits. Sometimes it can all happen | 12 |
| in just a few minutes, so be ready. If you are inside when a tornado hits, run | 29 |
| to the basement or a room with no windows. If you are in a car, stop under | 46 |
| an overpass. But no matter what you do, never try to outrun a tornado. | 60 |
| Some tornadoes form over lakes or seas. These are called "waterspouts." | 71 |
| They pull water high into the air. | 78 |
| In time, their winds slow down. The things and water they sucked* up | 91 |
| fall from the sky. This can also cause odd things to happen. | 103 |

**Chapter 6** *page 24*

| | |
|---|---:|
| *Back to the huge, slow-moving plates. Every so often, one plate | 11 |
| pushes on another one. The place where this happens is called a "fault line." | 25 |
| The two plates may not move at first. But the pushing goes on. It gets | 40 |
| stronger and stronger. Finally the plates move. When they move, an | 51 |
| earthquake happens. | 53 |
| When an earthquake hits, the ground begins to shake. It may become | 65 |
| very loud. Cars and trucks may turn over. Buildings may fall as big cracks | 79 |
| open up in the earth. | 84 |
| If you are ever in an* earthquake, stand in a doorway. This will help keep | 99 |
| things from falling on you. | 104 |

- The target rate for **The Unexpected** is 90 wcpm. The asterisks (*) mark 90 words.
- Listen to the student read the passage. Count the number of words read in one minute and the number of errors.
- For the reading rate, subtract the number of errors from the total number of words read.
- Have students enter their scores on their **Fluency Graph.** See page 9.

# Answer Key

## Building Background

Name _____ Date _____

*Master of Disaster*
**What You Know**
Write answers to these questions.

1. Use a dictionary to write the meaning of these words: *extreme, disaster, natural, man-made*. **the greatest degree; a happening that causes much damage or suffering; produced by nature, not by human beings; made by people, not by nature**

2. List eight different kinds of disasters, both natural and man-made. Circle the natural disasters. Put a box around the man-made ones.
   **Accept reasonable responses.**

3. What kinds of natural disasters have occurred in the region where you live? What safety rules did you follow during those disasters?
   **Answers will vary.**

### Word Meanings
*Synonyms*
Look for these words as you read your chapter book. When you find one of these words, write a synonym for it.

during: **in the course of, throughout**
huge: **colossal, immense**
nice: **enjoyable, pleasant**
push: **propel, thrust**
whole: **complete, full**
worse: **aggravate, inflame**

72 — The Unexpected • Book 6

*Master of Disaster*

---

## Chapter Quiz

Name _____ Date _____

*Master of Disaster*
**Chapter 1, "Tornadoes"**
Mark each statement *T* for true or *F* for false.

**T** 1. Tornadoes are often called "twisters."
**F** 2. Tornadoes are formed when hot air from the ground mixes with hot air in the sky.
**F** 3. Cold air from the ground pushes spinning air up.
**F** 4. Winds in a tornado can reach up to 900 miles an hour.
**F** 5. It is unusual for a tornado to pick up things as large as cars and houses.
**T** 6. One tornado sucked 30 cows into the sky, but the cows were not killed.
**F** 7. Tornadoes usually do not smash things to bits.
**T** 8. If you are home during a tornado, it is best to run to the basement.
**F** 9. If you are driving when a tornado hits, it is best to try to outrun the tornado.
**T** 10. *Waterspouts* are tornadoes that form over lakes or seas.

Read the question, and write your answer.

Why did it once rain fish in Rhode Island and toads in France?
**Waterspouts, tornadoes that form over water, sucked up the fish and the toads and dropped them over the land.**

74 — The Unexpected • Book 6

*Master of Disaster*

---

## Chapter Quiz

Name _____ Date _____

*Master of Disaster*
**Chapter 2, "The Big Heat"**
Fill in the bubble beside the answer for each question.

1. Heat in a city is worse than heat in a small town because
   Ⓐ tall buildings keep cool winds out.
   Ⓑ bricks and streets hold in the heat from sunlight.
   ● both A and B

2. Air "bumps" usually form over
   Ⓐ open fields.
   Ⓑ small towns.
   ● big cities.

3. You can stay cool at home by
   Ⓐ keeping the shades up during the day.
   ● drinking lots of water.
   Ⓒ not using the fan.

4. Which group of people is most at risk of getting sick from the heat?
   Ⓐ middle-aged people
   Ⓑ teenagers
   ● older people

Read the question, and write your answer.

What are three things you can do to stay cool in very hot weather?
**Ideas: stay in air-cooled buildings; go swimming; stay out of the sun; put on a hat; keep the fan on; drink lots of water; pull down the shades**

The Unexpected • Book 6 — 75

*Master of Disaster*

---

## Chapter Quiz

Name _____ Date _____

*Master of Disaster*
**Chapter 3, "C-C-Cold"**
Fill in the bubble beside the answer for each question.

1. Very cold weather can be
   ● just as bad as very hot weather.
   Ⓑ as cold as 10°F.
   Ⓒ not as bad with the wind blowing.

2. In very cold weather
   Ⓐ your face, hands, or feet can freeze.
   Ⓑ your skin can start to look like wax.
   ● both A and B

3. When your whole body gets too cold you
   ● shiver a lot.
   Ⓑ have lots of energy.
   Ⓒ both A and B

4. Cold-weather outfits
   Ⓐ should not be too heavy.
   ● should keep you dry and away from the wind.
   Ⓒ work better when they are wet.

Read the question, and write your answer.

Why is licking a metal pole in freezing weather a bad idea?
**Your tongue will freeze to the pole, and it will hurt a lot to get your tongue unstuck.**

76 — The Unexpected • Book 6

*Master of Disaster*

---

82      The Unexpected • Book 6

# Answer Key

## Chapter Quiz

Name _____ Date _____

*Master of Disaster*
**Chapter 4, "Storm Surges"**
**Number the events in order from 1 to 5.**

_4_ The water sank into the ground, leaving salt behind.
_2_ Seawater smashed buildings and flooded farms.
_1_ During Hurricane Katrina, huge waves went over the levees.
_5_ No plants will grow there for years and years.
_3_ Seawater killed most of the plants.

**Mark each statement T for true or F for false.**

_T_ 1. The disaster in New Orleans was the result of a hurricane combined with a flood.
_F_ 2. Seawater helps plants grow because of the salt.
_T_ 3. Hurricane Katrina was one of the worst disasters to happen in the United States.
_F_ 4. Removing the wetlands and building a harbor for ships was a good idea.

**Read the question, and write your answer.**

What had been done in New Orleans that made the damage from Hurricane Katrina worse than other storms?
**Wetlands between the city and the sea were removed to make way for ships. When Katrina hit, there were no wetlands to break up the big waves.**

The Unexpected • Book 6    77

## Chapter Quiz

Name _____ Date _____

*Master of Disaster*
**Chapter 5, "Tsunamis"**
**Number the events in order from 1 to 5.**

_2_ Shock waves moved through deep water and formed waves on top of the water.
_3_ Near the shore, the waves became huge walls of water.
_5_ In minutes, more than 250,000 people died.
_4_ The waves roared in and smashed everything in their path.
_1_ In 2004 there was an earthquake deep in the Indian Ocean.

**Mark each statement T for true or F for false.**

_F_ 1. Tidal waves are not the same as tsunamis.
_T_ 2. Tsunamis can be caused by earthquakes.
_T_ 3. A tsunami in Alaska was caused by a huge chunk of rock that fell into the water.
_F_ 4. The tsunami in Alaska killed many people.

**Read the question, and write your answer.**

What should you do if you are by the sea and the water suddenly leaves the shore and doesn't come back?
**Run as fast as you can for high ground. Do not stay near the shore.**

78    The Unexpected • Book 6

## Chapter Quiz

Name _____ Date _____

*Master of Disaster*
**Chapter 6, "Earthquakes"**
**Mark each statement T for true or F for false.**

_T_ 1. Earth is not hard all the way through.
_F_ 2. The mass of red-hot, melted rock is called the "crust."
_T_ 3. The continents lie on huge blocks of crust called "plates."
_F_ 4. The continents are moving several feet every year.
_F_ 5. If you are in an earthquake, you should stand beside a window.
_T_ 6. The biggest fault line in the United States is in California.
_F_ 7. The worst earthquake ever to hit the United States was in Northridge in 1994.
_T_ 8. Fighting fires after an earthquake can be very difficult because water mains can break during the earthquake.
_T_ 9. There are machines that can sense very tiny movements in Earth's crust.
_F_ 10. People are more likely than animals to know an earthquake is coming.

**Read the question, and write your answer.**

What causes an earthquake? Use the terms *mantle, crust,* and *plates* in your answer.
**Earth's crust floats on top of the mantle, which is red-hot, melted rock. The crust is broken up into 15 huge plates, which can push up against one another. The pushing gets harder and stronger until an earthquake hits.**

The Unexpected • Book 6    79

## Thinking and Writing

Name _____ Date _____

*Master of Disaster*
**Think About It**

Write about or give an oral presentation for each question.

1. Compare tornadoes with hurricanes. How are they alike? How are they different? **Tornadoes form over land, hurricanes form at sea, but both have high winds.**

2. How are natural and man-made disasters alike? How are they different? Which do you think are worse and why? **Accept reasonable responses.**

3. Make a list of extremes of nature this book tells about. For each extreme, describe how it affects people and list any warnings people may have. Which extreme would be easiest to avoid? **Accept reasonable answers.**

4. How could the damage to New Orleans from Hurricane Katrina, the heat extremes in cities, and the San Francisco earthquake be both man-made and natural disasters? **Idea: Man-made changes such as removing wetlands, building high buildings, and lots of people living close together made the disasters worse.**

**Write About It**

Choose one of the questions below. Write your answer on a sheet of paper.

1. Write a *Master of Disaster Safety Booklet* describing how to be safe in a tornado, a hurricane, extreme heat and cold, a tsunami, and an earthquake.

2. Pretend you lived through one of the natural disasters in this book. Write a letter telling what happened to you. Tell about any warning you had and how you protected yourself.

3. Complete the Content Web for this book.

80    The Unexpected • Book 6

The Unexpected • Book 6    83

# Building Background

Name _____ Date _____

## *The Legend of Sleepy Hollow*
## What You Know

**Write answers to these questions.**

1. What kinds of things do you think are scary? _____
_____

2. Why do you think people like scary stories, scary movies, or scary rides at amusement parks? _____
_____

3. What kinds of things do people do to impress their friends or show off their talents? _____
_____

4. Writers sometimes hint at what will happen later in a story. This is called "foreshadowing." Give an example of foreshadowing from a book, a movie, or a television show. _____
_____

## Word Meanings
### Definitions

**Look for these words as you read your chapter book. When you find one of these words, write its definition.**

haunted: _____

chattering: _____

legend: _____

tarry: _____

scared: _____

whistled: _____

# Word Lists

## The Legend of Sleepy Hollow

| Unfamiliar Words | Word Meanings | Proper Nouns | |
|---|---|---|---|
| afternoon, bridge, buried, courage, ghost, graveyard, scariest, schoolhouse, shadows, victim, wives | legend, tarry, whistled | Headless Horseman, Hudson River, Ichabod Crane, Sleepy Hollow, Tarry Town | Chapter 1 |
| favorite, hosts, husband, patched, place, skinny, study, thought, voice | scared | | Chapter 2 |
| castle, marry, race, reason, stronger, sure, taught, whenever | haunted | Brom Bones, Katrina van Tassel | Chapter 3 |
| burst, dance, elbow, grasshopper, music, pointed | | Daredevil, Gunpowder | Chapter 4 |
| church, circle, crept, instead, might, scary, snorted | chattering | | Chapter 5 |
| heart, married, owner, pumpkin, townspeople | | | Chapter 6 |

The Unexpected • Book 7

# Chapter Quiz

Name _____ Date _____

## *The Legend of Sleepy Hollow*
## Chapter 1, "A Ghost on Horseback!"

**Fill in the bubble beside the answer for each question.**

1. Where is Tarry Town?
   - Ⓐ along the Hudson River
   - Ⓑ in the sea
   - Ⓒ in the mountains

2. What was the name of the ghost?
   - Ⓐ Headless Horseman
   - Ⓑ Old Cannonball
   - Ⓒ Tarry Jones

3. How did the men feel when they went home at night?
   - Ⓐ happy to be walking
   - Ⓑ a little afraid
   - Ⓒ sad about leaving

4. What was the victim's name?
   - Ⓐ Sleepy Hollow
   - Ⓑ Ghost Rider
   - Ⓒ Ichabod Crane

**Read the question, and write your answer.**

In this chapter, we learn that there will be another story involving the Headless Horseman. What do you think it will be about?

_____

_____

# Chapter Quiz

Name _____ Date _____

## *The Legend of Sleepy Hollow*
### Chapter 2, "A New Teacher in Town"

**Mark each statement *T* for true or *F* for false.**

_____ 1. Ichabod looked like a big bird.

_____ 2. The school was a good place to study.

_____ 3. Ichabod was paid well.

_____ 4. Ichabod moved from one house to another.

_____ 5. People were sad when Ichabod left their houses.

_____ 6. Ichabod gave dancing lessons.

_____ 7. Women thought Ichabod would make a good husband.

_____ 8. Ichabod could not read.

_____ 9. Ichabod liked ghost stories.

_____ 10. Ichabod did not believe in ghosts.

**Read the question, and write your answer.**

Why do you think Ichabod believed in ghosts? _____

_____

# Chapter Quiz

Name _____ Date _____

## *The Legend of Sleepy Hollow*
### Chapter 3, "Mr. Crane's Girl"

**Fill in the bubble beside the answer for each question.**

1. Why did Ichabod go to Katrina's house?
   - Ⓐ to give her singing lessons
   - Ⓑ to read ghost stories to her
   - Ⓒ just to talk

2. What did he like best about Katrina?
   - Ⓐ her singing
   - Ⓑ her father's wealth
   - Ⓒ her looks

3. What did Ichabod decide to do?
   - Ⓐ leave town
   - Ⓑ stop teaching
   - Ⓒ win Katrina over

4. Why did other men stay away from Katrina?
   - Ⓐ Brom liked her.
   - Ⓑ They were afraid of her father.
   - Ⓒ Ichabod liked her.

**Read the question, and write your answer.**

How did Brom scare Ichabod? _____

_____

88                                    The Unexpected • Book 7

# Chapter Quiz

Name _____ Date _____

## *The Legend of Sleepy Hollow*
## Chapter 4, "The Big Party"

**Number the events in order from 1 to 5.**

____ Brom raced by Ichabod on his horse.

____ Ichabod got ready for the party.

____ Ichabod let class out early on the day of the party.

____ Ichabod got on Gunpowder.

____ Ichabod looked for Katrina when the music started.

**Number the events in order from 6 to 10.**

____ Katrina and Ichabod danced while Brom watched.

____ People started telling ghost stories.

____ Ichabod told about the haunted school.

____ The song ended, and people cheered.

____ Brom told about racing the Headless Horseman.

**Read the question, and write your answer.**

Why did some of the old men smile when Brom said he had met the Headless Horseman? _____

_____

_____

The Unexpected • Book 7

# Chapter Quiz

Name _____ Date _____

## *The Legend of Sleepy Hollow*
### Chapter 5, "The Victim"

**Number the events in order from 1 to 5.**

____ Ichabod thought about Brom's ghost story.

____ Ichabod tried to make the horse hurry.

____ Ichabod left the party in a gloomy mood.

____ Ichabod almost flipped over Gunpowder's head.

____ Gunpowder ran in a circle and stopped suddenly.

**Number the events in order from 6 to 10.**

____ The stranger threw his head at Ichabod.

____ When Ichabod yelled, Gunpowder started to run.

____ Ichabod saw a rider on a black horse.

____ Ichabod asked, "Who are you?"

____ The Horseman's head hit Ichabod's head.

**Read the question, and write your answer.**

Who do you think was dressed as the Headless Horseman? Why?

_____

_____

_____

# Chapter Quiz

Name _____ Date _____

## *The Legend of Sleepy Hollow*
### Chapter 6, "The Missing Teacher"

**Mark each statement *T* for true or *F* for false.**

_____ 1. No one saw Gunpowder again.

_____ 2. They found Ichabod near the bridge.

_____ 3. The students waited outside the school.

_____ 4. Everyone looked for Ichabod.

_____ 5. A farmer found Ichabod's hat.

_____ 6. Someone found a head near the bridge.

_____ 7. Farmers think a ghost killed Ichabod.

_____ 8. Brom married Katrina.

_____ 9. Katrina knew what had happened to Ichabod.

_____ 10. Brom felt bad about Ichabod.

**Read the question, and write your answer.**

What surprised you most about this book?

_____

_____

_____

The Unexpected • Book 7 — 91

# Thinking and Writing

Name _____ Date _____

## *The Legend of Sleepy Hollow*
### Think About It

**Write about or give an oral presentation for each question.**

1. What do you think happened to Ichabod? _____
   _____
   _____

2. What do you think is the best part of the story? _____
   _____
   _____

3. Setting is the place and the time of a story. Was the setting important in this story? Why or why not? _____
   _____
   _____

## Write About It

**Choose one of the questions below. Write your answer on a sheet of paper.**

1. List ways that Ichabod and Brom were different. Then use your list to write a comparison and contrast of the two men.

2. The story ends with a mystery. Write a new ending to the story.

3. Complete the Main Idea/Details Chart for this book.

92                                                    The Unexpected • Book 7

# Fluency Passages

## *The Legend of Sleepy Hollow*

**Chapter 1** *page 4*

| | |
|---|---:|
| *The wind carried the tale across the land. It said a soldier was buried | 14 |
| in the graveyard. He had lost his head in battle. Each night this "Headless | 28 |
| Horseman" rode through Sleepy Hollow, looking for his head. | 37 |
| | |
| On dark nights you could hear his horse on the old bridge. Before the | 51 |
| sun came up, the Headless Horseman went back across the bridge to the | 64 |
| graveyard. | 65 |
| | |
| People told many stories about this ghost. Some farmers laughed at | 76 |
| the stories. But when they walked home at night, they were silent as the* | 90 |
| shadows fell across their tracks. Some whistled a song for courage. | 101 |

**Chapter 5** *page 21*

| | |
|---|---:|
| *When Ichabod reached the road to Sleepy Hollow, Brom's ghost | 10 |
| story crept into his mind. He could not think of anything else. | 22 |
| | |
| Ichabod wanted to be brave. He tried to whistle. When he did, he | 35 |
| thought he heard his whistle answered. Or was it just the wind? He looked | 49 |
| into the night. Then he heard another scary sound. It was his own teeth | 63 |
| chattering! | 64 |
| | |
| Ichabod quickly kicked Gunpowder to get him to run. But the horse | 76 |
| was tired of taking orders. He jumped to the side and ran in a* circle. | 91 |
| | |
| Then he suddenly stopped. Ichabod almost flipped over the horse's | 101 |
| head. | 102 |

---

- The target rate for **The Unexpected** is 90 wcpm. The asterisks (*) mark 90 words.

- Listen to the student read the passage. Count the number of words read in one minute and the number of errors.

- For the reading rate, subtract the number of errors from the total number of words read.

- Have students enter their scores on their **Fluency Graph.** See page 9.

# Answer Key

## Building Background

Name _____ Date _____

*The Legend of Sleepy Hollow*
**What You Know**
Write answers to these questions.

1. What kinds of things do you think are scary? **Accept reasonable responses.**

2. Why do you think people like scary stories, scary movies, or scary rides at amusement parks? **Accept reasonable responses.**

3. What kinds of things do people do to impress their friends or show off their talents? **dress up, change hairstyles, perform publicly**

4. Writers sometimes hint at what will happen later in a story. This is called "foreshadowing." Give an example of foreshadowing from a book, a movie, or a television show. **Answers will vary.**

**Word Meanings**
*Definitions*
Look for these words as you read your chapter book. When you find one of these words, write its definition.

haunted: **cursed, visited by a ghost**
chattering: **clicking together repeatedly**
legend: **story handed down through the years**
tarry: **linger, hang around**
scared: **alarmed, frightened**
whistled: **made a shrill sound by blowing through pursed lips**

84     The Unexpected • Book 7

*The Legend of Sleepy Hollow*

---

## Chapter Quiz

Name _____ Date _____

*The Legend of Sleepy Hollow*
**Chapter 1, "A Ghost on Horseback!"**
Fill in the bubble beside the answer for each question.

1. Where is Tarry Town?
   - ● along the Hudson River
   - Ⓑ in the sea
   - Ⓒ in the mountains

2. What was the name of the ghost?
   - ● Headless Horseman
   - Ⓑ Old Cannonball
   - Ⓒ Tarry Jones

3. How did the men feel when they went home at night?
   - Ⓐ happy to be walking
   - ● a little afraid
   - Ⓒ sad about leaving

4. What was the victim's name?
   - Ⓐ Sleepy Hollow
   - Ⓑ Ghost Rider
   - ● Ichabod Crane

Read the question, and write your answer.

In this chapter, we learn that there will be another story involving the Headless Horseman. What do you think it will be about? **It will involve Ichabod Crane, who will become a victim of the Headless Horseman.**

86     The Unexpected • Book 7

*The Legend of Sleepy Hollow*

---

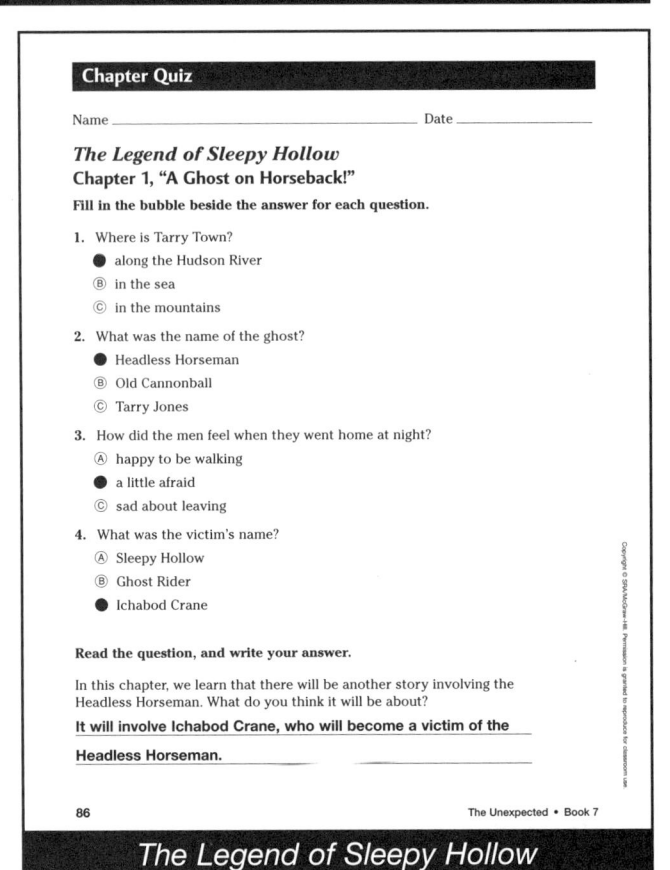

## Chapter Quiz

Name _____ Date _____

*The Legend of Sleepy Hollow*
**Chapter 2, "A New Teacher in Town"**
Mark each statement *T* for true or *F* for false.

- **T** 1. Ichabod looked like a big bird.
- **T** 2. The school was a good place to study.
- **F** 3. Ichabod was paid well.
- **T** 4. Ichabod moved from one house to another.
- **F** 5. People were sad when Ichabod left their houses.
- **F** 6. Ichabod gave dancing lessons.
- **T** 7. Women thought Ichabod would make a good husband.
- **F** 8. Ichabod could not read.
- **T** 9. Ichabod liked ghost stories.
- **F** 10. Ichabod did not believe in ghosts.

Read the question, and write your answer.
Why do you think Ichabod believed in ghosts? **Ideas: vivid imagination, lots of realistic stories, hard to prove stories were untrue**

The Unexpected • Book 7     87

*The Legend of Sleepy Hollow*

---

## Chapter Quiz

Name _____ Date _____

*The Legend of Sleepy Hollow*
**Chapter 3, "Mr. Crane's Girl"**
Fill in the bubble beside the answer for each question.

1. Why did Ichabod go to Katrina's house?
   - ● to give her singing lessons
   - Ⓑ to read ghost stories to her
   - Ⓒ just to talk

2. What did he like best about Katrina?
   - Ⓐ her singing
   - ● her father's wealth
   - Ⓒ her looks

3. What did Ichabod decide to do?
   - Ⓐ leave town
   - Ⓑ stop teaching
   - ● win Katrina over

4. Why did other men stay away from Katrina?
   - ● Brom liked her.
   - Ⓑ They were afraid of her father.
   - Ⓒ Ichabod liked her.

Read the question, and write your answer.

How did Brom scare Ichabod? **He broke into the school and turned all the desks around.**

88     The Unexpected • Book 7

*The Legend of Sleepy Hollow*

---

94     The Unexpected • Book 7

# Answer Key

---

**Chapter Quiz**

Name _____ Date _____

*The Legend of Sleepy Hollow*
**Chapter 4, "The Big Party"**

Number the events in order from 1 to 5.

- _4_ Brom raced by Ichabod on his horse.
- _2_ Ichabod got ready for the party.
- _1_ Ichabod let class out early on the day of the party.
- _3_ Ichabod got on Gunpowder.
- _5_ Ichabod looked for Katrina when the music started.

Number the events in order from 6 to 10.

- _6_ Katrina and Ichabod danced while Brom watched.
- _8_ People started telling ghost stories.
- _9_ Ichabod told about the haunted school.
- _7_ The song ended, and people cheered.
- _10_ Brom told about racing the Headless Horseman.

Read the question, and write your answer.

Why did some of the old men smile when Brom said he had met the Headless Horseman? **They knew Brom was making up a story to frighten Ichabod.**

*The Legend of Sleepy Hollow*

---

**Chapter Quiz**

Name _____ Date _____

*The Legend of Sleepy Hollow*
**Chapter 5, "The Victim"**

Number the events in order from 1 to 5.

- _2_ Ichabod thought about Brom's ghost story.
- _3_ Ichabod tried to make the horse hurry.
- _1_ Ichabod left the party in a gloomy mood.
- _5_ Ichabod almost flipped over Gunpowder's head.
- _4_ Gunpowder ran in a circle and stopped suddenly.

Number the events in order from 6 to 10.

- _9_ The stranger threw his head at Ichabod.
- _8_ When Ichabod yelled, Gunpowder started to run.
- _6_ Ichabod saw a rider on a black horse.
- _7_ Ichabod asked, "Who are you?"
- _10_ The Horseman's head hit Ichabod's head.

Read the question, and write your answer.

Who do you think was dressed as the Headless Horseman? Why? **Brom; to frighten Ichabod so he would leave the village and Brom could marry Katrina**

*The Legend of Sleepy Hollow*

---

**Chapter Quiz**

Name _____ Date _____

*The Legend of Sleepy Hollow*
**Chapter 6, "The Missing Teacher"**

Mark each statement *T* for true or *F* for false.

- _F_ 1. No one saw Gunpowder again.
- _F_ 2. They found Ichabod near the bridge.
- _T_ 3. The students waited outside the school.
- _T_ 4. Everyone looked for Ichabod.
- _T_ 5. A farmer found Ichabod's hat.
- _F_ 6. Someone found a head near the bridge.
- _F_ 7. Farmers think a ghost killed Ichabod.
- _T_ 8. Brom married Katrina.
- _F_ 9. Katrina knew what had happened to Ichabod.
- _F_ 10. Brom felt bad about Ichabod.

Read the question, and write your answer.

What surprised you most about this book?
**Answers will vary.**

*The Legend of Sleepy Hollow*

---

**Thinking and Writing**

Name _____ Date _____

*The Legend of Sleepy Hollow*
**Think About It**

Write about or give an oral presentation for each question.

1. What do you think happened to Ichabod? **Ideas: He ran away; he settled in another town.**

2. What do you think is the best part of the story? **Answers will vary. [Note: This is a good opportunity to discuss conflict, rising action, climax, and resolution.]**

3. Setting is the place and the time of a story. Was the setting important in this story? Why or why not? **Ideas: Yes, the setting is a lonely, scary bridge near a graveyard; yes, a long time ago people told ghost stories for entertainment.**

**Write About It**

Choose one of the questions below. Write your answer on a sheet of paper.

1. List ways that Ichabod and Brom were different. Then use your list to write a comparison and contrast of the two men.

2. The story ends with a mystery. Write a new ending to the story.

3. Complete the Main Idea/Details Chart for this book.

*The Legend of Sleepy Hollow*

---

The Unexpected • Book 7     95

# Building Background

Name _____ Date _____

## *King Midas and the Golden Touch*
## What You Know

**Write answers to these questions.**

1. Research and describe how a modern-day king lives, compared to his subjects. Write your answer on a separate piece of paper.

2. What do you think it would be like to live in a royal palace?

   _____

   _____

3. What is greed? Give at least one example. _____

   _____

   _____

4. Do you think money can make people happy? Explain your answer.

   _____

   _____

# Word Meanings
## Synonyms

**Look for these words as you read your chapter book. When you find one of these words, write a synonym for it.**

foolish: _____

wise: _____

oracle: _____

sign: _____

touch: _____

# Word Lists

## *King Midas and the Golden Touch*

| Unfamiliar Words | Word Meanings | Proper Nouns | |
|---|---|---|---|
| child<br>coin<br>count<br>crown<br>daughter<br>music<br>palace<br>rosebud<br>snapped | foolish<br>oracle<br>sign<br>touch | Kali [KAY-lee]<br>King Midas<br>Phrygia [FRIS-ee-ah] | Chapter 1 |
| god<br>guest<br>sure<br>thought | wise | Dionysus [deye-oh-NEYE-sus]<br>Greek<br>Silenus [seye-LEE-nus] | Chapter 2 |
| blankets<br>enjoy<br>great<br>heart<br>true | | | Chapter 3 |
| attendant<br>happily<br>knife<br>napkin<br>piece<br>thankful<br>threw | | | Chapter 4 |
| stomach<br>tear<br>untouched | | | Chapter 5 |
| face<br>learned<br>nightfall<br>pitcher<br>refilled<br>servant<br>simple<br>statue<br>wrote | | | Chapter 6 |

The Unexpected • Book 8     97

# Chapter Quiz

Name _____  Date _____

## *King Midas and the Golden Touch*
### Chapter 1, "The King's Two Loves"

**Fill in the bubble beside the answer for each question.**

1. What did the ants put on Midas's lips?
   - Ⓐ grains of wheat
   - Ⓑ grains of sand
   - Ⓒ grains of gold

2. Whom did Midas's family ask about this sign?
   - Ⓐ a king
   - Ⓑ some ants
   - Ⓒ an oracle

3. What did Midas love most?
   - Ⓐ gold and power
   - Ⓑ gold and Kali
   - Ⓒ his crown and his palace

4. Where did Midas and Kali walk together?
   - Ⓐ by a creek
   - Ⓑ in a rose garden
   - Ⓒ to a town

**Read the question, and write your answer.**

Why do you think Midas named his daughter Kali?

_____

_____

The Unexpected • Book 8

# Chapter Quiz

Name _____  Date _____

## *King Midas and the Golden Touch*
### Chapter 2, "A Wish"

**Number the events in order from 1 to 5.**

___ Kali saw an old man asleep in the roses.

___ Midas and Kali showed Silenus his bed.

___ Midas woke the man and asked who he was.

___ Midas asked Silenus to come in and eat.

___ Silenus said he was on his way to see Dionysus but got lost.

**Number the events in order from 6 to 10.**

___ Silenus left to find Dionysus.

___ Dionysus said Midas was foolish.

___ Silenus stayed with King Midas for ten days.

___ Midas wished for the golden touch.

___ Dionysus went to see Midas to grant him a wish.

**Read the question, and write your answer.**

Why does Dionysus tell Midas he is a foolish man?

_____

_____

# Chapter Quiz

Name _____ Date _____

## *King Midas and the Golden Touch*
### Chapter 3, "The Good"

**Mark each statement *T* for true or *F* for false.**

_____ 1. Midas heard Dionysus's warning.

_____ 2. Midas was afraid to try the golden touch.

_____ 3. Midas started by touching small things.

_____ 4. Midas felt lucky.

_____ 5. Midas's heart beat faster because he was angry.

_____ 6. Kali watched her father turn things to gold.

_____ 7. Dionysus watched Midas turn things to gold.

_____ 8. Everything Midas touched turned to gold.

_____ 9. Midas was happy with the golden touch.

_____ 10. Midas turned the palace into gold.

**Read the question, and write your answer.**

What do you think will happen in the next chapter?

_____

_____

# Chapter Quiz

Name _____ Date _____

## *King Midas and the Golden Touch*
### Chapter 4, "The Bad"

**Mark each statement *T* for true or *F* for false.**

____ 1. Midas was too happy to be hungry.

____ 2. Midas could not wait to use his golden touch at dinner.

____ 3. The knife, plate, and cup turned to gold.

____ 4. The meat and water turned to gold.

____ 5. Midas could eat if a servant fed him.

____ 6. The servant was afraid of Midas's golden touch.

____ 7. Kali ate dinner with Midas.

____ 8. Midas threw his napkin because he was angry.

____ 9. The golden touch was not all good.

____ 10. The golden touch worked just as Midas thought it would.

**Read the question, and write your answer.**

At what point in this chapter does Midas realize that the golden touch might be bad?

_____

_____

The Unexpected • Book 8

# Chapter Quiz

Name _____ Date _____

## *King Midas and the Golden Touch*
### Chapter 5, "The Lesson"

**Number the events in order from 1 to 5.**

____ Midas told his stomach to stop growling.

____ The rose turned to gold.

____ Midas bent over to smell a rose.

____ Midas walked through the palace.

____ Midas sat on a golden bench in the rose garden.

**Number the events in order from 6 to 10.**

____ Midas was sad that he could not smell the roses.

____ Kali turned into a golden statue.

____ Kali came up behind Midas and tugged on his arm.

____ Midas turned all the roses to gold.

____ Midas wanted to get rid of the golden touch.

**Read the question, and write your answer.**

Midas loves two things above all others; how do these two things change?

_____

_____

**Chapter Quiz**

Name _____ Date _____

## *King Midas and the Golden Touch*
### Chapter 6, "No More Golden Touch"

**Fill in the bubble beside the answer for each question.**

1. To whom did Midas write?
   - Ⓐ an oracle
   - Ⓑ Silenus
   - Ⓒ Dionysus

2. Why did Midas think he would die?
   - Ⓐ He could not sleep.
   - Ⓑ He could not eat.
   - Ⓒ Kali was a statue.

3. What did Midas learn?
   - Ⓐ Gold is not all good.
   - Ⓑ Simple things are better than gold.
   - Ⓒ both A and B

4. What was the first thing Midas put water on?
   - Ⓐ Kali
   - Ⓑ a rose
   - Ⓒ the palace

**Read the question, and write your answer.**

What does this story tell us about the Greek god Dionysus?

_____

_____

The Unexpected • Book 8

# Thinking and Writing

Name _____ Date _____

## *King Midas and the Golden Touch*
### Think About It

**Write about or give an oral presentation for each question.**

1. A myth tells about people who lived a long time ago and about their gods. Describe the Greek god Dionysus. _____
_____
_____

2. "Take time to smell the roses." Midas learned that lesson. What do you think this saying means? Is it good advice? Why? _____
_____
_____

3. Do you think Midas became a better king after he lost his golden touch? Why or why not? _____
_____
_____

## Write About It

**Choose one of the questions below. Write your answer on a sheet of paper.**

1. Pretend you are Kali. Write two pages in your journal. Write one page about life before the golden touch. Write the next page about life after Midas got rid of the golden touch. Make sure you tell your feelings about the golden touch.

2. Find another myth, and read it. Write a report about the myth. At the end of your report, tell which myth you like better and why.

3. Complete the Book Report Form for this book.

104     The Unexpected • Book 8

# Fluency Passages

## King Midas and the Golden Touch

**Chapter 4** *page 19*

| | |
|---|---:|
| *"Water!" Midas said. "Please give me a drink of water." | 10 |
| The attendant picked up the cup. Her hands shook as she lifted it. As | 24 |
| soon as the water touched the king's lips, it turned to gold. | 36 |
| The attendant dropped the cup. "Don't touch me!" she yelled at Midas. | 48 |
| Then she ran out of the room. | 55 |
| Midas picked up the napkin that lay next to his plate. It turned to gold. | 70 |
| Midas threw the napkin to the floor. It landed with a thud. He got up. | 85 |
| "Maybe a walk in my* rose garden will take my mind off food," he | 99 |
| said. | 100 |

**Chapter 5** *page 21*

| | |
|---|---:|
| *He got up and bent over a rose. He sniffed the flower. It turned to | 15 |
| gold. He bent and touched another rose with his nose. Gold! | 26 |
| "It's clear to me now," he said. "The golden touch is not just in my | 41 |
| fingers. Making a garden of gold will help me forget my hunger." | 53 |
| Midas walked in the garden, touching each rose. There were many | 64 |
| roses. It took him a long time. But turning the roses to gold made him feel | 80 |
| good. He even forgot about his hunger. | 87 |
| Then Midas noted* something bad. He could not smell the roses. | 98 |

---

- The target rate for **The Unexpected** is 90 wcpm. The asterisks (*) mark 90 words.
- Listen to the student read the passage. Count the number of words read in one minute and the number of errors.
- For the reading rate, subtract the number of errors from the total number of words read.
- Have students enter their scores on their **Fluency Graph.** See page 9.

The Unexpected • Book 8

# Answer Key

## Building Background

Name _____ Date _____

*King Midas and the Golden Touch*
**What You Know**
Write answers to these questions.

1. Research and describe how a modern-day king lives, compared to his subjects. Write your answer on a separate piece of paper.
   **Kings and queens usually live in palaces and lead wealthy lives.**
2. What do you think it would be like to live in a royal palace?
   **Accept reasonable responses.**
3. What is greed? Give at least one example. **Greed is a selfish desire for more than you need without considering the needs of others; accept reasonable examples.**
4. Do you think money can make people happy? Explain your answer.
   **Accept reasonable responses.**

**Word Meanings**
*Synonyms*
Look for these words as you read your chapter book. When you find one of these words, write a synonym for it.

foolish: **senseless, silly**
wise: **aware, all-knowing**
oracle: **fortune teller, prophet**
sign: **warning, forewarning**
touch: **feel, stroke**

96 — The Unexpected • Book 8
*King Midas and the Golden Touch*

---

## Chapter Quiz

Name _____ Date _____

*King Midas and the Golden Touch*
**Chapter 1, "The King's Two Loves"**
Fill in the bubble beside the answer for each question.

1. What did the ants put on Midas's lips?
   ● grains of wheat
   Ⓑ grains of sand
   Ⓒ grains of gold

2. Whom did Midas's family ask about this sign?
   Ⓐ a king
   Ⓑ some ants
   ● an oracle

3. What did Midas love most?
   Ⓐ gold and power
   ● gold and Kali
   Ⓒ his crown and his palace

4. Where did Midas and Kali walk together?
   Ⓐ by a creek
   ● in a rose garden
   Ⓒ to a town

Read the question, and write your answer.

Why do you think Midas named his daughter Kali?
**Kali means "rosebud"; she was named after something Midas loved almost as much as gold.**

98 — The Unexpected • Book 8
*King Midas and the Golden Touch*

---

## Chapter Quiz

Name _____ Date _____

*King Midas and the Golden Touch*
**Chapter 2, "A Wish"**
Number the events in order from 1 to 5.

**1** Kali saw an old man asleep in the roses.
**5** Midas and Kali showed Silenus his bed.
**2** Midas woke the man and asked who he was.
**4** Midas asked Silenus to come in and eat.
**3** Silenus said he was on his way to see Dionysus but got lost.

Number the events in order from 6 to 10.

**7** Silenus left to find Dionysus.
**10** Dionysus said Midas was foolish.
**6** Silenus stayed with King Midas for ten days.
**9** Midas wished for the golden touch.
**8** Dionysus went to see Midas to grant him a wish.

Read the question, and write your answer.

Why does Dionysus tell Midas he is a foolish man?
**Ideas: Midas does not take time to think about his request; he does not understand what he is asking for.**

The Unexpected • Book 8 — 99
*King Midas and the Golden Touch*

---

## Chapter Quiz

Name _____ Date _____

*King Midas and the Golden Touch*
**Chapter 3, "The Good"**
Mark each statement *T* for true or *F* for false.

**F** 1. Midas heard Dionysus's warning.
**F** 2. Midas was afraid to try the golden touch.
**T** 3. Midas started by touching small things.
**T** 4. Midas felt lucky.
**F** 5. Midas's heart beat faster because he was angry.
**F** 6. Kali watched her father turn things to gold.
**F** 7. Dionysus watched Midas turn things to gold.
**T** 8. Everything Midas touched turned to gold.
**T** 9. Midas was happy with the golden touch.
**T** 10. Midas turned the palace into gold.

Read the question, and write your answer.

What do you think will happen in the next chapter?
**Accept reasonable responses.**

100 — The Unexpected • Book 8
*King Midas and the Golden Touch*

---

106     The Unexpected • Book 8

# Answer Key

---

**Chapter Quiz**

Name _____ Date _____

*King Midas and the Golden Touch*
**Chapter 4, "The Bad"**
Mark each statement *T* for true or *F* for false.

- **F** 1. Midas was too happy to be hungry.
- **T** 2. Midas could not wait to use his golden touch at dinner.
- **T** 3. The knife, plate, and cup turned to gold.
- **T** 4. The meat and water turned to gold.
- **F** 5. Midas could eat if a servant fed him.
- **T** 6. The servant was afraid of Midas's golden touch.
- **F** 7. Kali ate dinner with Midas.
- **T** 8. Midas threw his napkin because he was angry.
- **T** 9. The golden touch was not all good.
- **F** 10. The golden touch worked just as Midas thought it would.

Read the question, and write your answer.

At what point in this chapter does Midas realize that the golden touch might be bad?
**when food turns to gold; when the servant cannot feed him**

*The Unexpected • Book 8*  101

*King Midas and the Golden Touch*

---

**Chapter Quiz**

Name _____ Date _____

*King Midas and the Golden Touch*
**Chapter 5, "The Lesson"**
Number the events in order from 1 to 5.

- **2** Midas told his stomach to stop growling.
- **5** The rose turned to gold.
- **4** Midas bent over to smell a rose.
- **1** Midas walked through the palace.
- **3** Midas sat on a golden bench in the rose garden.

Number the events in order from 6 to 10.

- **7** Midas was sad that he could not smell the roses.
- **9** Kali turned into a golden statue.
- **8** Kali came up behind Midas and tugged on his arm.
- **6** Midas turned all the roses to gold.
- **10** Midas wanted to get rid of the golden touch.

Read the question, and write your answer.

Midas loves two things above all others; how do these two things change?
**Midas lost his love for gold when he turned Kali, the other thing he loved most, into a golden statue.**

102  *The Unexpected • Book 8*

*King Midas and the Golden Touch*

---

**Chapter Quiz**

Name _____ Date _____

*King Midas and the Golden Touch*
**Chapter 6, "No More Golden Touch"**
Fill in the bubble beside the answer for each question.

1. To whom did Midas write?
   - Ⓐ an oracle
   - Ⓑ Silenus
   - ● Dionysus

2. Why did Midas think he would die?
   - Ⓐ He could not sleep.
   - ● He could not eat.
   - Ⓒ Kali was a statue.

3. What did Midas learn?
   - Ⓐ Gold is not all good.
   - Ⓑ Simple things are better than gold.
   - ● both A and B

4. What was the first thing Midas put water on?
   - ● Kali
   - Ⓑ a rose
   - Ⓒ the palace

Read the question, and write your answer.

What does this story tell us about the Greek god Dionysus?
**kind, thoughtful, generous, caring, capable of doing the impossible**

*The Unexpected • Book 8*  103

*King Midas and the Golden Touch*

---

**Thinking and Writing**

Name _____ Date _____

*King Midas and the Golden Touch*
**Think About It**
Write about or give an oral presentation for each question.

1. A myth tells about people who lived a long time ago and about their gods. Describe the Greek god Dionysus. **Ideas: The gods in Greek myths are like people. Dionysus looked like a person but had special powers.**

2. "Take time to smell the roses." Midas learned that lesson. What do you think this saying means? Is it good advice? Why?
**Idea: If you hurry too much, you miss happy experiences.**

3. Do you think Midas became a better king after he lost his golden touch? Why or why not? **Ideas: Yes, Midas learned that some things are worth more than gold; no, Midas did not learn from his mistakes.**

**Write About It**

Choose one of the questions below. Write your answer on a sheet of paper.

1. Pretend you are Kali. Write two pages in your journal. Write one page about life before the golden touch. Write the next page about life after Midas got rid of the golden touch. Make sure you tell your feelings about the golden touch.

2. Find another myth, and read it. Write a report about the myth. At the end of your report, tell which myth you like better and why.

3. Complete the Book Report Form for this book.

104  *The Unexpected • Book 8*

*King Midas and the Golden Touch*

---

*The Unexpected • Book 8*  107

# Graphic Organizer

Name _____ Date _____

## *Making Gold*
### Story Grammar Map

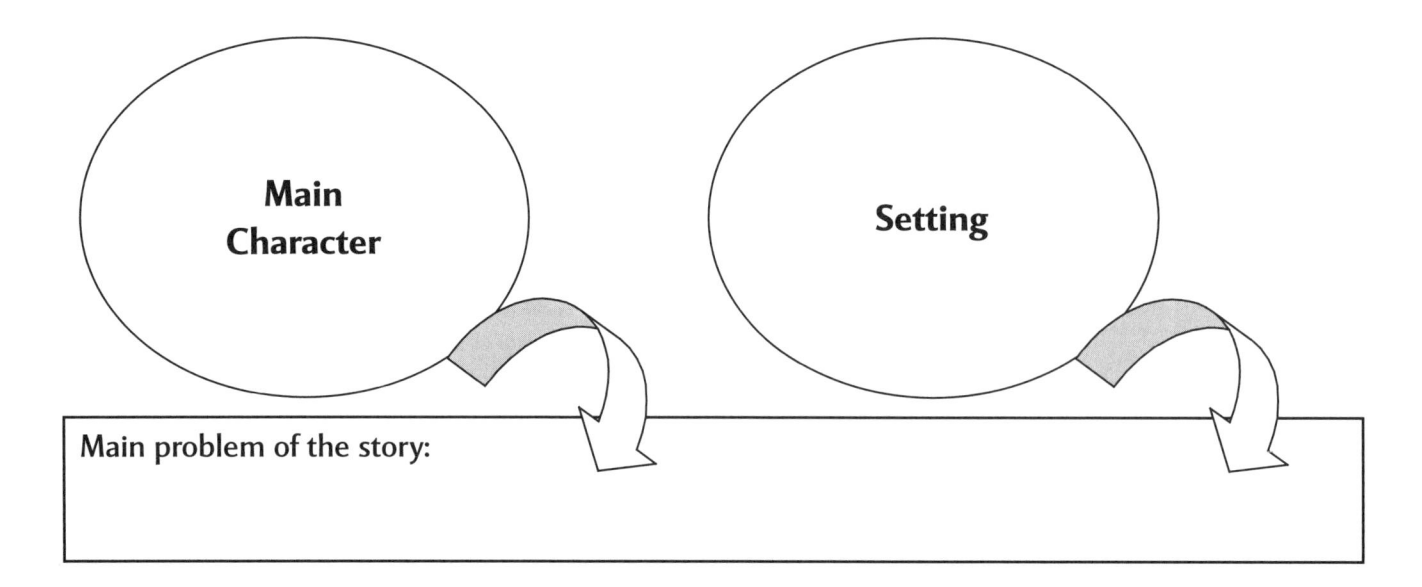

( Main Character )    ( Setting )

Main problem of the story:

An event in the story:

An event in the story:

How was the story's problem solved?

What is the ending?

108　　　　　　　　　　　　　　　　　　　　　　　The Unexpected

**Graphic Organizer**

Name _____ Date _____

# *Born Dead: The Story of Gordon Parks*
## Sequencing Chart

**List steps or events in time order (in the order they occurred in the story).**

| |
|---|
| Topic: |
| First: |
| Next: |
| Next: |
| Next: |
| Next: |
| Next: |
| Next: |
| Finally: |

The Unexpected

# Graphic Organizer

Name _____ Date _____

## *The Navel of the World*
**What I Know/What I Learned Chart**

| What I Know | What I Want to Know | What I Learned |
|---|---|---|
|  |  |  |

**Graphic Organizer**

Name _____  Date _____

## *The Mountain Is on Fire!*
### Compare and Contrast Diagram

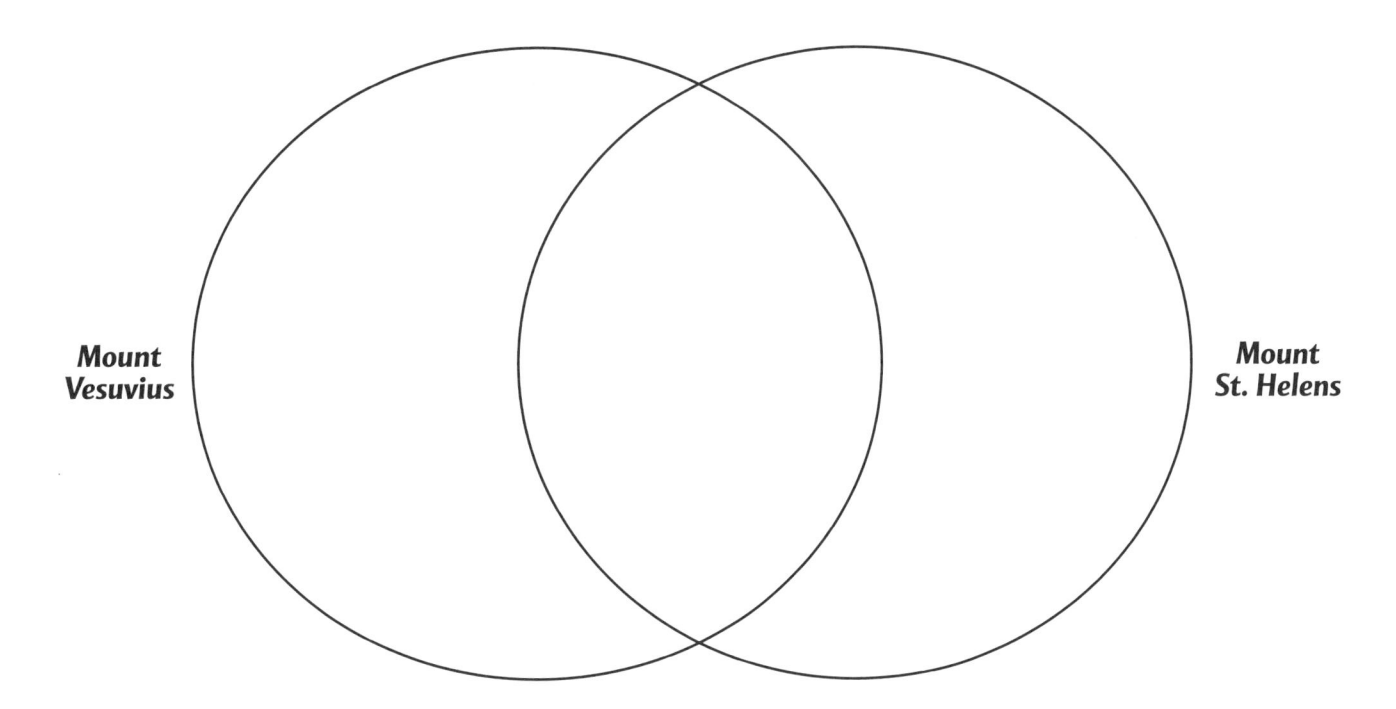

**Mount Vesuvius**     **Mount St. Helens**

- What is **different** about Mount Vesuvius goes in the circle on the left.
- What is **different** about Mount St. Helens goes in the circle on the right.
- What is the **same about both** goes in the overlapping area in the middle.

The Unexpected

# Graphic Organizer

Name _____ Date _____

## *Atlantis: Land of Mystery*
### Genres Chart

| Reality (fact) | Fantasy (fiction) |
|---|---|
|  |  |

# Graphic Organizer

Name _____ Date _____

## *Master of Disaster*
## Content Web

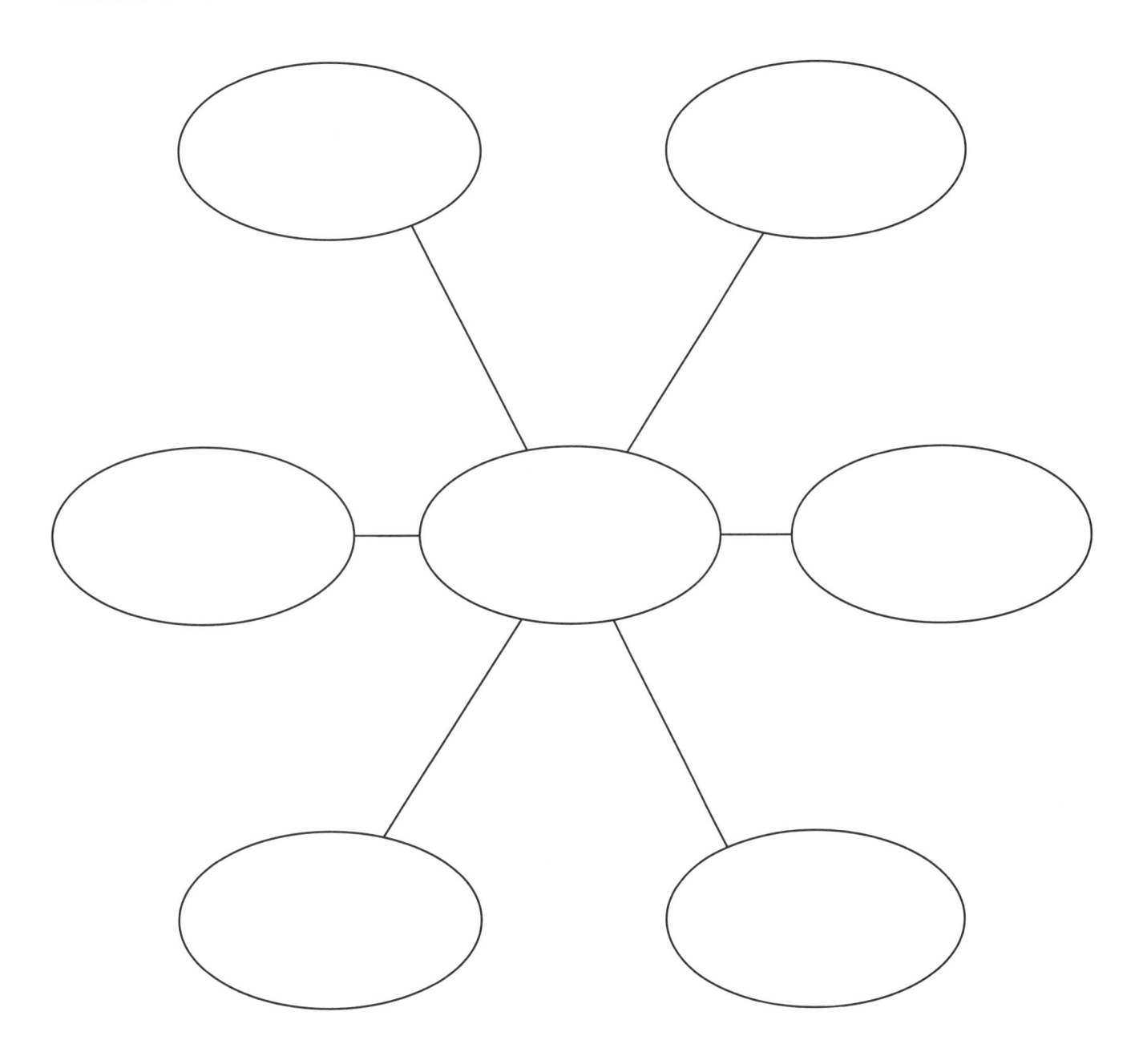

The Unexpected

113

# Graphic Organizer

Name _____  Date _____

## *The Legend of Sleepy Hollow*
**Main Idea/Details Chart**

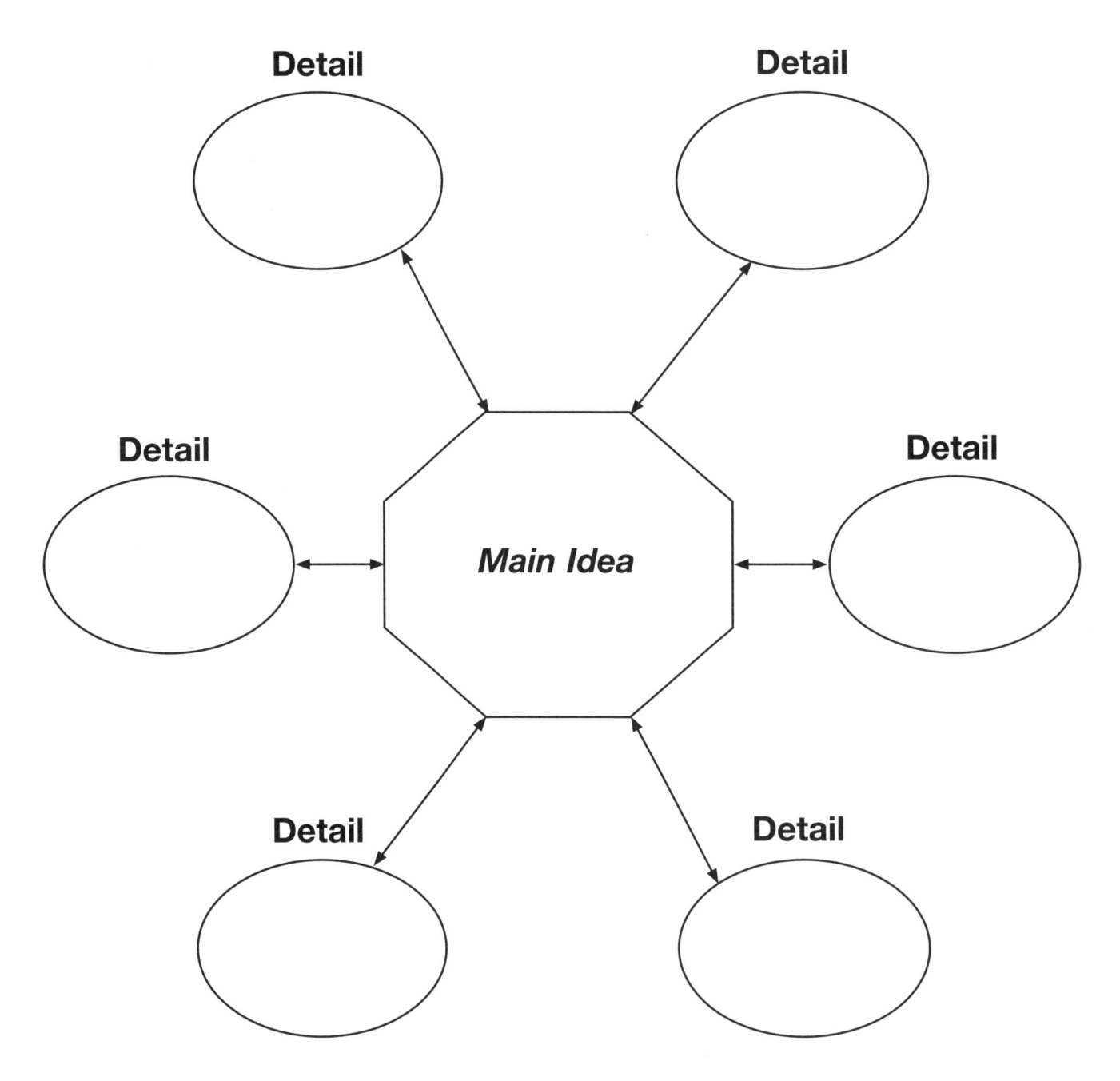

Detail

Detail

Detail

Detail

Detail

Detail

Main Idea

The Unexpected

# Graphic Organizer

Name _____ Date _____

## *King Midas and the Golden Touch*
### Book Report Form

Describe the main character from your book by writing descriptions in the boxes as needed.

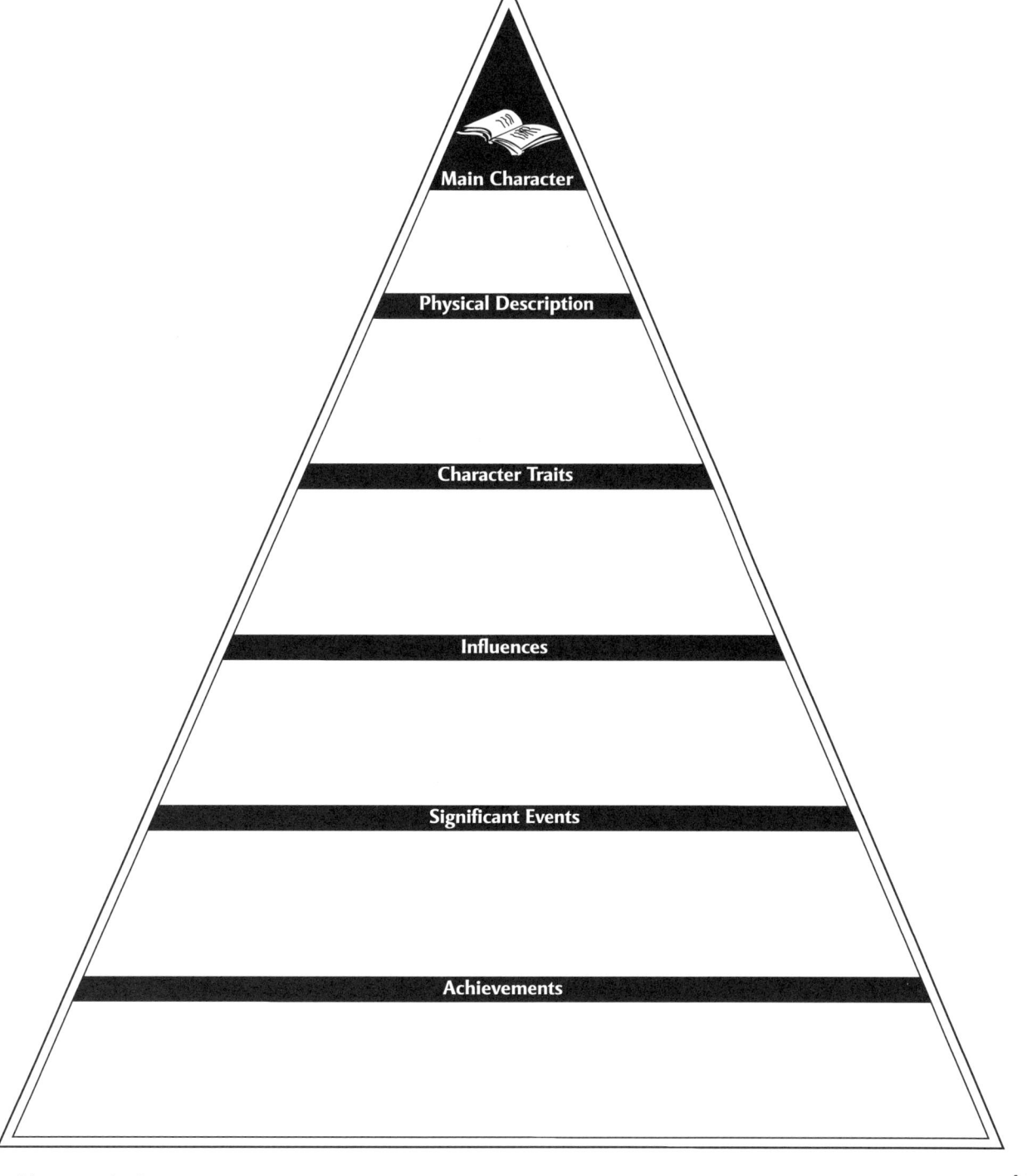

- Main Character
- Physical Description
- Character Traits
- Influences
- Significant Events
- Achievements

The Unexpected